CONSTITUTIONAL LAW FOR A CHANGING AMERICA

RIGHTS, LIBERTIES, AND JUSTICE

1997–1999 SUPPLEMENT

LEE EPSTEIN
WASHINGTON UNIVERSITY

THOMAS G. WALKER
EMORY UNIVERSITY

CQ PRESS

A DIVISION OF CONGRESSIONAL QUARTERLY INC.
WASHINGTON, D.C.

CQ Press
A Division of Congressional Quarterly Inc.
1414 22nd Street, N.W.
Washington, DC 20037

(202) 822-1475; (800) 638-1710

www.cqpress.com

Printed in the United States of America

Library of Congress Cataloging-in-Publication Data

in process

CONTENTS

During its 1997–1999 terms, the Supreme Court issued eight decisions that have important implications for the rights and liberties of all Americans. Three of these, *Arkansas Educational Television Commission v. Forbes* (1998), *National Endowment for the Arts v. Finley* (1998), and *Greater New Orleans Broadcasting Association, Inc. v. United States* (1999), centered on the First Amendment. In *Forbes*, the justices were asked to determine whether the First Amendment permits a television station to refuse the request of a duly qualified candidate for public office to participate in a televised candidate debate. The question in *Finley* was no less significant: May the government consider general standards of decency in deciding which arts projects to fund? Finally, in *Greater New Orleans Broadcasting*, the Court continued its exploration of commercial speech, addressing questions associated with broadcast advertising of lotteries and casino gambling.

Four cases focused on matters of criminal justice but raised distinct issues. In *Campbell v. Louisiana* (1998), the justices considered whether white defendants have standing to object to discrimination against blacks in the selection of grand jurors. In *Pennsylvania Board of Probation and Parole v. Scott* (1998), they addressed the question whether unconstitutionally gathered evidence should be used in a judicial proceeding. In *Wilson v. Lane* (1999), which also involved issues pertaining to the use of evidence, the question was whether, under the Fourth Amendment, police may invite representatives of the media to accompany them (a so-called "media ride-along") when they are executing a warrant. Finally, in *City of Chicago v. Morales* (1999), the Court considered whether an anti-loitering ordinance, aimed at curtailing street-gang crime, violates individual rights.

The remaining dispute concerned discrimination, specifically the question whether states can pay lower welfare benefits to new residents. The Court addressed this important matter in *Saenz v. Roe* (1999). Despite the differences among these disputes, they all illustrate how constitutional amendments drafted more than two hundred years ago continue to shape the contours of our rights and liberties today. Students wishing to read the full text of the Supreme Court opinions excerpted in this supplement will find them in the official *United States Reports*, available in all law libraries and at many college and public libraries. The opinions are also available on the Internet. Navigate to: *http:// supct.law.cornell.edu/supct/index.html.*

CHAPTER 5

FREEDOM OF SPEECH, ASSEMBLY, AND ASSOCIATION

REGULATING PUBLIC TELEVISION

Throughout its history the Supreme Court has taken the general position that increased political expression is valued under the First Amendment. As long as the manner of expression remains peaceful and otherwise conforms to the general constitutional limitations, more expression is to be preferred to less. However, the government on occasion may attempt to restrict equal access to expression opportunities. Are such restrictions consistent with the First Amendment? This question is addressed in *Arkansas Educational Television Commission v. Forbes* (1998). Here the Court wrestles with the question whether the First Amendment permits the administrators of a state-operated television station to refuse the request of a duly qualified candidate for public office to participate in a televised candidate debate.

Arkansas Educational Television Commission v. Forbes

_____ U.S. _____ (1998)

Vote: 6 *(Breyer, Kennedy, O'Connor, Rehnquist, Scalia, Thomas)*
    3 *(Ginsburg, Souter, Stevens)*
Opinion of the Court: Kennedy
Dissenting Opinion: Stevens

The Arkansas Educational Television Commission (AETC) is a state agency that owns and operates a network of five public television stations. Members of the commission are appointed by the governor for eight-year terms. The commission employs a professional executive director and a staff who exercise broad editorial discretion in planning the network's programming. The network adheres to generally accepted broadcast industry standards of operation.

In 1992 the commission sponsored a series of televised debates among candidates for various elective offices, including the Third Congressional District of Arkansas. Ralph Forbes, running as an independent for the seat, was a perennial candidate who had sought, without success, several elective posts. When he learned that the list of debate participants included only Democratic and Republican candidates, Forbes wrote the commission asking to be included. The executive director replied that a journalistic decision had been made to limit the debate to viable candidates. Three days before the debate, Forbes sued, claiming his exclusion from the debate violated his First Amendment freedom of speech rights. While the courts took up the issue, the debate went on without Forbes's participation.

The district court ruled in favor of the commission, holding that his exclusion was reasonable. The court of appeals, however, reversed, finding that the state did not have a compelling interest to limit the debate to viable candidates. The commission requested a review by the Supreme Court.

JUSTICE KENNEDY delivered the opinion of the Court.

A state-owned public television broadcaster sponsored a candidate debate from which it excluded an independent candidate with little popular support. The issue before us is whether, by reason of its state ownership, the station had a constitutional obligation to allow every candidate access to the debate. We conclude that, unlike most other public television programs, the candidate debate was subject to constitutional constraints applicable to nonpublic fora under our forum precedents. Even so, the broadcaster's decision to exclude the candidate was a reasonable, viewpoint-neutral exercise of journalistic discretion. . . .

[T]he issue is whether [Forbes's] exclusion from the debate was consistent with the First Amendment. The Court of Appeals held it was not, applying our public forum precedents. Appearing as amicus curiae in support of petitioners, the Solicitor General argues that our forum precedents should be of little relevance in the context of television broadcasting. At the outset, then, it is instructive to ask whether public forum principles apply to the case at all.

Having first arisen in the context of streets and parks, the public forum doctrine should not be extended in a mechanical way to the very different context of public television broadcasting. In the case of streets and parks, the open access and viewpoint neutrality commanded by the doctrine is "compatible with the intended purpose of the property." *Perry Ed. Assn. v. Perry Local Educators' Assn.* (1983). So too was the requirement of viewpoint neutrality compatible with the university's funding of student publications in *Rosenberger v. Rector and Visitors of Univ. of Va.* (1995). In the case of television broadcasting, however, broad rights of access for outside speakers would be antithetical, as a general rule, to the discretion that stations and their editorial staff must exercise to fulfill their journalistic purpose and statutory obligations.

Congress has rejected the argument that "broadcast facilities should be open on a nonselective basis to all persons wishing to talk about public issues." *Columbia Broadcasting System, Inc. v. Democratic National Committee* (1973). Instead, television broadcasters enjoy the "widest journalistic freedom" consistent with their public responsibilities. . . .

As a general rule, the nature of editorial discretion counsels against subjecting broadcasters to claims of viewpoint discrimination. Programming decisions would be particularly vulnerable to claims of this type because even principled exclusions rooted in sound journalistic judgment can often be characterized as viewpoint-based. To comply with their obligation to air programming that serves the public interest, broadcasters must often choose among speakers expressing different viewpoints. . . . Were the judiciary to require, and so to define and approve, pre-established criteria for access, it would risk implicating the courts in judgments that should be left to the exercise of journalistic discretion. . . .

Although public broadcasting as a general matter does not lend itself to scrutiny under the forum doctrine, candidate debates present the narrow exception to the rule. For two reasons, a candidate debate like the one at issue here is different from other programming. First, unlike AETC's other broadcasts, the debate was by design a forum for political speech by the candidates. Consistent with the long tradition of candidate debates, the implicit representation of the broadcaster was that the views expressed were those of the candidates, not its own. . . .

Second, in our tradition, candidate debates are of exceptional significance in the electoral process. . . . A majority of the population cites television as its primary source of election information, and debates are regarded as the "only occasion during a campaign when the attention of a large portion of the American public is focused on the election, as well as the only campaign information format which potentially offers sufficient time to explore issues and policies in depth in a neutral forum." Congressional Research Service (June 15, 1993).

As we later discuss, in many cases it is not feasible for the broadcaster to allow unlimited access to a candidate debate. Yet the requirement of neutrality remains; a broadcaster cannot grant or deny access to a candidate debate on the basis of whether it agrees with a candidate's views. Viewpoint discrimination in this context would present not a "[c]alculated ris[k]," *Columbia Broadcasting System, Inc.,* but an inevitability of skewing the electoral dialogue.

The special characteristics of candidate debates support the conclusion that the AETC debate was a forum of some type. The question of what type must be answered by reference to our public forum precedents, to which we now turn.

Forbes argues, and the Court of Appeals held, that the debate was a public forum to which he had a First Amendment right of access. Under our precedents, however, the debate was a nonpublic forum, from which AETC could exclude Forbes in the reasonable, viewpoint-neutral exercise of its journalistic discretion. For our purposes, it will suffice to employ the categories of speech fora already established and discussed in our cases. "[T]he Court [has] identified three types of fora: the traditional public forum, the public forum created by government designation, and the nonpublic forum." *Cornelius v. NAACP Legal Defense & Ed. Fund, Inc.* (1985). Traditional public fora are defined by the objective characteristics of the property, such as whether, "by long tradition or by government fiat," the property has been "devoted to assembly and debate." *Perry Ed. Assn.* The government can exclude a speaker from a traditional public forum "only when the exclusion is necessary to serve a compelling state interest and the exclusion is narrowly drawn to achieve that interest." *Cornelius.*

Designated public fora, in contrast, are created by purposeful governmental action. "The government does not create a [designated] public forum by inaction or by permitting limited discourse, but only by intentionally opening a nontraditional public forum for public discourse.". . . If the government excludes a speaker who falls within the class to which a designated public forum is made generally available, its action is subject to strict scrutiny.

Other government properties are either nonpublic fora or not fora at all. The government can restrict access to a nonpublic forum "as long as the restrictions are reasonable and [are] not an effort to suppress expression merely because public officials oppose the speaker's view." *Cornelius.*

In summary, traditional public fora are open for expressive activity regardless of the government's intent. The objective characteristics of these properties require the government to accommodate private speakers. The government is free to open additional properties for expressive use by the general public or by a particular class of speakers, thereby creating designated public fora. Where the property is not a traditional public forum and the government has not chosen to create a designated public forum, the property is either a nonpublic forum or not a forum at all.

The parties agree the AETC debate was not a traditional public forum. . . . [T]he almost unfettered access of a traditional public forum would be incompatible with the programming dictates a television broadcaster must follow. The issue, then, is whether the debate was a designated public forum or a nonpublic forum.

Under our precedents, the AETC debate was not a designated public forum. To create a forum of this type, the government must intend to make the property "generally available," *Widmar v. Vincent* (1981), to a class of speakers. In *Widmar,* for example, a state university created a public forum for registered student groups by implementing a policy that expressly made its meeting facilities "generally open" to such groups. A designated public forum is not created when the government allows selective access for individual speakers rather than general access for a class of speakers. In *Perry,* for example, the Court held a school district's internal mail system was not a designated public forum even though selected speakers were able to gain access to it. . . .

These cases illustrate the distinction between "general access," which indicates the property is a designated public forum, and "selective access," which indicates the property is a nonpublic forum. On one hand, the government creates a designated public forum when it makes its property generally available to a certain class of speakers, as the university made its facilities generally available to student groups in *Widmar.* On the other hand, the government does not create a designated public forum when it does no more than reserve eligibility for access to the forum to a particular class of speakers, whose members must then, as individuals, "obtain permission" to use it. For instance, the Federal Government did not create a designated public forum in *Cornelius* when it reserved eligibility for participation in the CFC [Combined Federal Campaign] drive to charitable agencies, and then made individual, non-ministerial judgments as to which of the eligible agencies would participate.

The *Cornelius* distinction between general and selective access furthers First Amendment interests. By recognizing the distinction, we encourage the government to open its property to some expressive activity in cases where, if faced with an all-or-nothing choice, it might not open the property at all. That this distinction turns on governmental intent does not render it unprotective of speech. Rather, it reflects the reality that, with the exception of traditional public fora, the government retains the choice of whether to designate its property as a forum for specified classes of speakers.

Here, the debate did not have an open-microphone format. Contrary to the assertion of the Court of Appeals, AETC did not make its debate generally available to candidates for Arkansas' Third Congressional District seat. . . . AETC made candidate-by-candidate determinations as to which of the eligible candidates would participate in the debate. "Such selective access, unsupported by evidence of a purposeful designation for public use, does not create a public forum." *Cornelius.* Thus the debate was a nonpublic forum.

In addition to being a misapplication of our precedents, the Court of Appeals' holding would result in less speech, not more. In ruling that the debate was a public forum open to all ballot-qualified candidates the Court of Appeals would place a severe burden upon public broadcasters who air candidates' views. . . .

Were it faced with the prospect of cacophony, on the one hand, and First Amendment liability, on the other, a public television broadcaster might choose not to air candidates' views at all. A broadcaster might decide " ' the safe course is to avoid controversy,' . . . and by so doing diminish the free flow of information and ideas." *Turner Broadcasting System, Inc. [v. FCC]* (1994). In this circumstance, a "[g]overnment-enforced right of access inescapably 'dampens the vigor and limits the variety of public debate.' " Ibid. (quoting *New York Times Co. v. Sullivan* (1964)). . . .

The debate's status as a nonpublic forum, however, did not give AETC unfettered power to exclude any candidate it wished. . . . To be consistent with the First

Amendment, the exclusion of a speaker from a nonpublic forum must not be based on the speaker's viewpoint and must otherwise be reasonable in light of the purpose of the property. *Cornelius.*

In this case, the jury found Forbes' exclusion was not based on "objections or opposition to his views." The record provides ample support for this finding, demonstrating as well that AETC's decision to exclude him was reasonable. AETC Executive Director Susan Howarth testified Forbes' views had "absolutely" no role in the decision to exclude him from the debate. She further testified Forbes was excluded because (1) "the Arkansas voters did not consider him a serious candidate"; (2) "the news organizations also did not consider him a serious candidate"; (3) "the Associated Press and a national election result reporting service did not plan to run his name in results on election night"; (4) Forbes "apparently had little, if any, financial support, failing to report campaign finances to the Secretary of State's office or to the Federal Election Commission"; and (5) "there [was] no 'Forbes for Congress' campaign headquarters other than his house." Forbes himself described his campaign organization as "bedlam" and the media coverage of his campaign as "zilch." It is, in short, beyond dispute that Forbes was excluded not because of his viewpoint but because he had generated no appreciable public interest.

There is no substance to Forbes' suggestion that he was excluded because his views were unpopular or out of the mainstream. His own objective lack of support, not his platform, was the criterion. . . .

Nor did AETC exclude Forbes in an attempted manipulation of the political process. The evidence provided powerful support for the jury's express finding that AETC's exclusion of Forbes was not the result of "political pressure from anyone inside or outside [AETC]." There is no serious argument that AETC did not act in good faith in this case. AETC excluded Forbes because the voters lacked interest in his candidacy, not because AETC itself did.

The broadcaster's decision to exclude Forbes was a reasonable, viewpoint-neutral exercise of journalistic discretion consistent with the First Amendment. The judgment of the Court of Appeals is

Reversed.

JUSTICE STEVENS, with whom JUSTICE SOUTER and JUSTICE GINSBURG join, dissenting.

The Court has decided that a state-owned television network has no "constitutional obligation to allow every candidate access to" political debates that it sponsors. I do not challenge that decision. The judgment of the Court of Appeals should nevertheless be affirmed. The official action that led to the exclusion of respondent Forbes from a debate with the two major-party candidates for election to one of Arkansas' four seats in Congress does not adhere to well-settled constitutional principles. The ad hoc decision of the staff of the Arkansas Educational Television Commission (AETC) raises precisely the concerns addressed by "the many decisions of this Court over the last 30 years, holding that a law subjecting the exercise of First Amendment freedoms to the prior restraint of a license, without narrow, objective, and definite standards to guide the licensing authority, is unconstitutional." *Shuttlesworth v. Birmingham* (1969).

In its discussion of the facts, the Court barely mentions the standardless character of the decision to exclude Forbes from the debate. In its discussion of the law, the Court understates the constitutional importance of the distinction between state ownership and private ownership of broadcast facilities. . . .

AETC is a state agency whose actions "are fairly attributable to the State and subject to the Fourteenth Amendment, unlike the actions of privately owned broadcast licensees." The AETC staff members therefore "were not ordinary journalists: they were employees of government.". . .

. . . Because AETC is owned by the State, deference to its interest in making ad hoc decisions about the political content of its programs necessarily increases the risk of government censorship and propaganda in a way that protection of privately owned broadcasters does not.

The Court recognizes that the debates sponsored by AETC were "by design a forum for political speech by the candidates." The Court also acknowledges the central importance of candidate debates in the electoral process. Thus, there is no need to review our cases expounding on the public forum doctrine to conclude that the First Amendment will not tolerate a state agency's arbitrary exclusion from a debate forum based, for example, on an expectation that the speaker might be critical of the Governor, or might hold unpopular views about abortion or the death penalty. . . . The dispositive issue in this case, then, is not whether AETC created a designated public forum or a nonpublic forum, as the Court concludes, but whether AETC defined the contours of the debate forum with sufficient specificity to justify the exclusion of a ballot-qualified candidate. . . .

AETC's control was comparable to that of a local government official authorized to issue permits to use public facilities for expressive activities. In cases concerning access to a traditional public forum, we have found an analogy between the power to issue permits and the censorial power to impose a prior restraint on speech. . . .

. . . Given the special character of political speech, particularly during campaigns for elected office, the debate forum implicates constitutional concerns of the highest order, as the majority acknowledges. Indeed, the planning and management of political debates by state-owned broadcasters raise serious constitutional concerns that are seldom replicated when state-owned television networks engage in other types of programming. . . .

The reasons that support the need for narrow, objective, and definite standards to guide licensing decisions apply directly to the wholly subjective access decisions made by the staff of AETC.

The importance of avoiding arbitrary or viewpoint-based exclusions from political debates militates strongly in favor of requiring the controlling state agency to use (and adhere to) pre-established, objective criteria to determine who among qualified candidates may participate. When the demand for speaking facilities exceeds supply, the State must "ration or allocate the scarce resources on some acceptable neutral principle." *Rosenberger.* A constitutional duty to use objective standards—i.e., "neutral principles"—for determining whether and when to adjust a debate format would impose only a modest requirement that would fall far short of a duty to grant every multiple-party request. Such standards would also have the benefit of providing the public with some assurance that state-owned broadcasters cannot select debate participants on arbitrary grounds. Like the Court, I do not endorse the view of the Court of Appeals that all candidates who qualify for a position on the ballot are necessarily entitled to access to any state-sponsored debate. I am convinced, however, that the constitutional imperatives that motivated our decisions in cases like *Shuttlesworth* command that access to political debates planned and managed by state-owned entities be governed by pre-established, objective criteria. . . .

Accordingly, I would affirm the judgment of the Court of Appeals.

GOVERNMENT SUPPORT OF THE ARTS

The First Amendment protects more than just expression that is generally accepted by the population. In fact, the First Amendment was especially intended to protect unpopular messages that might be particularly vulnerable to government oppression. As a consequence, speakers, writers, artists, politicians, and others are free to express views that the majority might reject. Their expressions may be disrespectful, offensive, and indecent and still merit First Amendment protection. While there are conditions that justify regulation—for example, a breakdown in public order or obscenity—the First Amendment does not permit discrimination based on the content of the expression. The foregoing assumes that the individuals or groups expressing such views are doing so at their own initiative or expense. But do these general rules change if government is financially supporting the expression? May the government set standards for public support that take into consideration factors that would be illegitimate in a regulatory statute? That issue came before the Court in *National Endowment for the Arts v. Finley* (1998), a challenge to the criteria used by the NEA in funding artistic expression.

National Endowment for the Arts v. Finley

_____ U.S. _____ (1998)

Vote: 8 (Breyer, Ginsburg, Kennedy, O'Connor, Rehnquist, Scalia, Stevens, Thomas)
*   1 (Souter)*
Opinion of the Court: O'Connor
Concurring Opinion: Scalia
Dissenting Opinion: Souter

Congress established the National Endowment for the Arts in 1965 as part of a general policy of supporting the arts through federal grants. Applications for NEA funding are reviewed first by advisory panels of experts, who make recommendations to a National Council on the Arts, which in turn advises the NEA chair. The chair has the ultimate authority to award grants, but he or she may not fund projects that receive negative recommendations from the council. Between 1965 and 1998, the NEA awarded more than $3 billion to support various arts initiatives. These funds went to state arts agencies, symphony orchestras, fine arts museums, opera associations, and individuals.

In 1989 two projects that received support from the NEA caused public controversy. The first was a retrospective of photographer Robert Mapplethorpe's work, parts of which many thought were obscene. The second was a photograph by artist Andres Serrano depicting a crucifix immersed in urine. The public controversy over federal money being used to support such projects prompted Congress in 1990 to revise its regulations governing the NEA. Among these revisions was section 954(d)(1) of the Arts and Humanities Act which directs the chair, in establishing procedures to judge the artistic merit of grant applications, to take into consideration "general standards of decency and respect for the diverse beliefs and values of the American public."

Four performance artists, including Karen Finley, applied for NEA funding before section 954(d)(1) was enacted. An advisory panel recommended approval of the projects, but a majority of the council recommended disapproval. The four sued the NEA claiming, among other things, that the agency violated the artists' First Amendment rights by denying their applications on political grounds. Shortly thereafter, when Congress passed section 954(d)(1), they amended their suit to challenge the new regulations for violating the First Amendment and for being unconstitutionally vague. The district court ruled in favor of the artists, and a divided court of appeals affirmed.

JUSTICE O'CONNOR delivered the opinion of the Court.

Respondents raise a facial constitutional challenge to §954(d)(1), and consequently they confront "a heavy burden" in advancing their claim. . . . To prevail, respondents must demonstrate a substantial risk that application of the provision will lead to the suppression of speech.

Respondents argue that the provision is a paradigmatic example of viewpoint discrimination because it rejects any artistic speech that either fails to respect mainstream values or offends standards of decency. The premise of respondents' claim is that §954(d)(1) constrains the agency's ability to fund certain categories of artistic expression. The NEA, however, reads the provision as merely hortatory, and contends that it stops well short of an absolute restriction. Section 954(d)(1) adds "considerations" to the grant-making process; it does not preclude awards to projects that might be deemed "indecent" or "disrespectful," nor place conditions on grants, or even specify that those factors must be given any particular weight in reviewing an application. Indeed, the agency asserts that it has adequately implemented §954(d)(1) merely by ensuring the representation of various backgrounds and points of view on the advisory panels that analyze grant applications. We do not decide whether the NEA's view—that the formulation of diverse advisory panels is sufficient to comply with Congress' command—is in fact a reasonable reading of the statute. It is clear, however, that the text of §954(d)(1) imposes no categorical requirement. The advisory language stands in sharp contrast to congressional efforts to prohibit the funding of certain classes of speech. When Congress has in fact intended to affirmatively constrain the NEA's grant-making authority, it has done so in no uncertain terms. See §954(d)(2) ("[O]bscenity is without artistic merit, is not protected speech, and shall not be funded").

Furthermore, like the plain language of §954(d), the political context surrounding the adoption of the "decency and respect" clause is inconsistent with respondents' assertion that the provision compels the NEA to deny funding on the basis of viewpoint discriminatory criteria. The legislation was a bipartisan proposal introduced as a counterweight to amendments aimed at eliminating the NEA's funding or substantially constraining its grant-making authority.. . . . [T]he criteria in §954(d)(1) inform the assessment of artistic merit, but Congress declined to disallow any particular viewpoints. . . . In contrast, before the vote on §954(d)(1), one of its sponsors stated: "If we have done one important thing in this amendment, it is this. We have maintained the integrity of freedom of expression in the United States."

That §954(d)(1) admonishes the NEA merely to take "decency and respect" into consideration, and that the legislation was aimed at reforming procedures rather than precluding speech, undercut respondents' argument that the provision inevitably will be utilized as a tool for invidious viewpoint discrimination. In cases where we have struck down legislation as facially unconstitutional, the dangers were both more evident and more substantial. In *R. A. V. v. St. Paul* (1992), for example, we invalidated on its face a municipal ordinance that defined as a criminal offense the placement of a symbol on public or private property " 'which one knows or has reasonable grounds to know arouses anger, alarm, or resentment in others on the basis of race, color, creed, religion, or gender.' " That provision set forth a clear penalty, proscribed views on particular "disfavored subjects," and suppressed "distinctive idea[s], conveyed by a distinctive message."

In contrast, the "decency and respect" criteria do not silence speakers by expressly "threaten[ing] censorship of ideas." Thus, we do not perceive a realistic danger that §954(d)(1) will compromise First Amendment values. . . .

Respondents' claim that the provision is facially unconstitutional may be reduced to the argument that the criteria in §954(d)(1) are sufficiently subjective that the agency could utilize them to engage in viewpoint discrimination. Given the varied interpretations of the criteria and the vague exhortation to "take them into consideration," it seems unlikely that this provision will introduce any greater element of selectivity than the determination of "artistic excellence" itself. And we are reluctant, in any event, to invalidate legislation "on the basis of its hypothetical application to situations not before the Court.". . .

Respondents do not allege discrimination in any particular funding decision. Thus, we have no occasion here to address an as-applied challenge in a situation where the denial of a grant may be shown to be the product of invidious viewpoint discrimination. If the NEA were to leverage its power to award subsidies on the basis of subjective criteria into a penalty on disfavored viewpoints, then we would confront a different case. . . . Unless and until §954(d)(1) is applied in a manner that raises concern about the suppression of disfavored viewpoints, however, we uphold the constitutionality of the provision.

Finally, although the First Amendment certainly has application in the subsidy context, we note that the Government may allocate competitive funding according to criteria that would be impermissible were direct regulation of speech or a criminal penalty at stake. So long as legislation does not infringe on other constitutionally protected rights, Congress has wide latitude to set spending priorities. . . .

The lower courts also erred in invalidating §954(d)(1) as unconstitutionally vague. Under the First and Fifth Amendments, speakers are protected from arbitrary and discriminatory enforcement of vague standards. . . .

In the context of selective subsidies, it is not always feasible for Congress to legislate with clarity. Indeed, if this statute is unconstitutionally vague, then so too are all government programs awarding scholarships and grants on the basis of subjective criteria such as "excellence.". . .

Section 954(d)(1) merely adds some imprecise considerations to an already subjective selection process. It does not, on its face, impermissibly infringe on First or Fifth Amendment rights. Accordingly, the judgment of the Court of Appeals is reversed and the case is remanded for further proceedings consistent with this opinion.

It is so ordered.

JUSTICE SCALIA, with whom JUSTICE THOMAS joins, concurring in the judgment.

"The operation was a success, but the patient died." What such a procedure is to medicine, the Court's opinion in this case is to law. It sustains the constitutionality of 20 U.S.C. § 954(d)(1) by gutting it. The most avid congressional opponents of the provision could not have asked for more. I write separately because, unlike the Court, I think that §954(d)(1) must be evaluated as written, rather than as distorted by the agency it was meant to control. By its terms, it establishes content- and viewpoint-based criteria upon which grant applications are to be evaluated. And that is perfectly constitutional. . . .

The phrase "taking into consideration general standards of decency and respect for the diverse beliefs and values of the American public" is what my grammar-school teacher would have condemned as a dangling modifier: There is no noun to which the participle is attached. Even so, it is clear enough that the phrase is meant to apply to those who do the judging. The application reviewers must take into account "general standards of decency" and "respect for the diverse beliefs and values of the American public" when evaluating artistic excellence and merit. One can regard this as either suggesting that decency and respect are elements of what Congress regards as artistic excellence and merit, or as suggesting that decency and respect are factors to be taken into account in addition to artistic excellence and merit. But either way, it is entirely, 100% clear that decency and respect are to be taken into account in evaluating applications.

This is so apparent that I am at a loss to understand what the Court has in mind (other than the gutting of the statute) when it speculates that the statute is merely "advisory.". . .

The Court devotes so much of its opinion to explaining why this statute means something other than what it says that it neglects to cite the constitutional text governing our analysis. The First Amendment reads: "Congress shall make no law . . . abridging the freedom of speech." To abridge is "to contract, to diminish; to deprive of." T. Sheridan, *A Complete Dictionary of the English Language* (6th ed. 1796). With the enactment of §954(d)(1), Congress did not abridge the speech of those who disdain the beliefs and values of the American public, nor did it abridge indecent speech. Those who wish to create indecent and disrespectful art are as unconstrained now as they were before the enactment of this statute. Avant-garde artistes such as respondents remain entirely free to épater les bourgeois; they are merely deprived of the additional satisfaction of having the bourgeoisie taxed to pay for it. It is preposterous to equate the denial of taxpayer subsidy with measures " ' "aimed at the suppression of dangerous ideas." ' " *Regan v. Taxation with Representation of Wash.* (1983). . . .

Section 954(d)(1) is no more discriminatory, and no less constitutional, than virtually every other piece of funding legislation enacted by Congress. "The Government can, without violating the Constitution, selectively fund a program to encourage certain activities it believes to be in the public interest, without at the same time funding an alternative program. . . ." *Rust v. Sullivan* (1991). . . .

The nub of the difference between me and the Court is that I regard the distinction between "abridging" speech and funding it as a fundamental divide, on this side of which the First Amendment is inapplicable. The Court, by contrast, seems to believe that the First Amendment, despite its words, has some ineffable effect upon funding, imposing constraints of an indeterminate nature which it announces (without troubling to enunciate any particular test) are not violated by the statute here—or, more accurately, are not violated by the quite different, emasculated statute that it imagines. . . .

Finally, what is true of the First Amendment is also true of the constitutional rule against vague legislation: it has no application to funding. Insofar as it bears upon First Amendment concerns, the vagueness doctrine addresses the problems that arise from government regulation of expressive conduct, see *Grayned v. City of Rockford* (1972), not government grant programs. In the former context, vagueness produces an abridgment of lawful speech; in the latter it produces, at worst, a waste of money. I cannot refrain from observing, however, that if the vagueness doctrine were applicable, the agency charged with making grants under a statutory standard of "artistic excellence"—and which has itself thought that standard met by everything from the playing of Beethoven to a depiction of a crucifix immersed in urine—would be of more dubious constitutional validity than the "decency" and "respect" limitations that respondents (who demand to be judged on the same strict standard of "artistic excellence") have the humorlessness to call too vague. . . .

. . . I concur only in the judgment.

Justice Souter, dissenting.

The decency and respect proviso mandates viewpoint-based decisions in the disbursement of government subsidies, and the Government has wholly failed to explain why the statute should be afforded an exemption from the fundamental rule of the First Amendment that viewpoint discrimination in the exercise of public authority over expressive activity is unconstitutional. The Court's conclusions that the proviso is not viewpoint based, that it is not a regulation, and that the NEA may permissibly engage in viewpoint-based discrimination, are all patently mistaken. . . .

"If there is a bedrock principle underlying the First Amendment, it is that the government may not prohibit the expression of an idea simply because society finds the idea itself offensive or disagreeable." *Texas v. Johnson* (1989). "[A]bove all else, the First Amendment means that government has no power to restrict expression because of its message [or] its ideas," *Police Dept. of Chicago v. Mosley* (1972), which is to say that "[t]he principle of viewpoint neutrality . . . underlies the First Amendment," *Bose Corp. v. Consumers Union of United States, Inc.* (1984). Because this principle applies not only to affirmative suppression of speech, but also to disqualification for government favors, Congress is generally not permitted to pivot discrimination against otherwise protected speech on the offensiveness or unacceptability of the views it expresses. . . .

When called upon to vindicate this ideal, we characteristically begin by asking "whether the government has adopted a regulation of speech because of disagreement with the message it conveys. The government's purpose is the controlling consideration." *Ward v. Rock Against Racism* [1989]. The answer in this case is damning. One need do nothing more than read the text of the statute to conclude that Congress's purpose in imposing the decency and respect criteria was to prevent the funding of art that conveys an offensive message; the decency and respect provision on its face is quintessentially viewpoint based, and quotations from the Congressional Record merely confirm the obvious legislative purpose. In the words of a cosponsor of the bill that enacted the proviso, "[w]orks which deeply offend the sensibilities of significant portions of the public ought not to be supported with public funds." Another supporter of the bill observed that "the Endowment's support for artists like Robert Mapplethorpe and Andre[s] Serrano has offended and angered many citizens," behooving "Congress . . . to listen to these complaints about the NEA and make sure that exhibits like [these] are not funded again." Indeed, if there were any question at all about what Congress had in mind, a definitive answer comes in the succinctly accurate remark of the proviso's author, that the bill "add[s] to the criteria of artistic excellence and artistic merit, a shell, a screen, a viewpoint that must be constantly taken into account.". . . .

Just as self-evidently, a statute disfavoring speech that fails to respect America's "diverse beliefs and values" is the very model of viewpoint discrimination; it penalizes any view disrespectful to any belief or value espoused by someone in the American populace. Boiled down to its practical essence, the limitation obviously means that art that disrespects the ideology, opinions, or convictions of a significant segment of the American public is to be disfavored, whereas art that reinforces those values is not. After all, the whole point of the proviso was to make sure that works like Serrano's ostensibly blasphemous portrayal of Jesus would not be funded, while a reverent treatment, conventionally respectful of Christian sensibilities, would not run afoul of the law. Nothing could be more viewpoint based than that. The fact that the statute disfavors art insufficiently respectful of America's "diverse" beliefs and values alters this conclusion not one whit: the First Amendment does not validate the ambition to disqualify many disrespectful viewpoints instead of merely one. . . .

Since the decency and respect proviso of §954(d)(1) is substantially overbroad and carries with it a significant power to chill artistic production and display, it should be struck down on its face.

REGULATING COMMERCIAL EXPRESSION

Historically, courts have viewed commercial expression as more closely related to commerce than to speech. Government has an interest in regulating fraudulent or deceptive messages that may be found in advertisements.

In addition, the subject matter of commercial expression is substantially different from the political and social speech at the heart of First Amendment protections. For these reasons, the courts have allowed more extensive government regulation of commercial expression than of other forms of speech. This principle was articulated in *Valentine v. Chrestensen* (1942), in which the Court upheld a law banning the distribution of handbills that advertised commercial goods and services. The Court concluded that the First Amendment does not protect "purely commercial advertising."

Beginning in the mid-1970s, however, the justices handed down decisions that indicated a reconsideration of the constitutional status of commercial expression. The general lesson we can draw from these cases is that governments have difficult standards to meet when they attempt to regulate nondeceptive commercial speech that concerns a lawful product or service.

Would this trend continue or even escalate to the point to which constitutional protections for commercial and noncommercial speech are indistinguishable? *Greater New Orleans Broadcasting Association, Inc. v. United States* (1999) provides some answers.

Greater New Orleans Broadcasting Association, Inc. v. United States

_____ U.S. _____ (1999)
Vote: 9 (Breyer, Ginsburg, Kennedy, O'Connor, Rehnquist, Scalia, Souter, Stevens, Thomas)
    0
Opinion of the Court: Stevens
Concurring Opinions: Rehnquist, Thomas

In 1934, Congress passed the Communications Act of 1934 (18 U.S.C. §1304), which prohibits broadcast advertising of lotteries and casino gambling. Subsequent years, however, brought exemptions to this blanket prohibition. For example, in response to the growing popularity of state-run lotteries, Congress exempted advertisements of such lotteries from broadcast restrictions when "broadcast by a radio and television station licensed to a location in . . . a State which conducts such a lottery." More recently, the 1988 Indian Gaming Regulatory Act exempts any "gaming" conducted by Native American tribes from the broadcast restrictions in the Communications Act.

The petitioners in this case are the Greater New Orleans Broadcasting Association and its members who operate radio and television stations in New Orleans. They would like to broadcast ads for casinos in Louisiana and Mississippi but cannot not do so in light of §1304 and various regulations enacted by the Federal Communications Commission pursuant to §1304. According to an FCC official, "Under appropriate conditions, some broadcast signals from Louisiana broadcasting stations may be heard in neighboring states including Texas and Arkansas," where private casino gambling is unlawful.

JUSTICE STEVENS delivered the opinion of the Court.

Federal law prohibits some, but by no means all, broadcast advertising of lotteries and casino gambling. In *United States v. Edge Broadcasting Co.* (1993), we upheld the constitutionality of 18 U.S.C. §1304 as applied to broadcast advertising of Virginia's lottery by a radio station located in North Carolina, where no such lottery was authorized. Today we hold that §1304 may not be applied to advertisements of private casino gambling that are broadcast by radio or television stations located in Louisiana, where such gambling is legal. . . .

In a number of cases involving restrictions on speech that is "commercial" in nature, we have employed *Central Hudson's* four-part test to resolve First Amendment challenges:

"At the outset, we must determine whether the expression is protected by the First Amendment. For commercial speech to come within that provision, it at least must concern lawful activity and not be misleading. Next, we ask whether the asserted governmental interest is substantial. If both inquiries yield positive answers, we must determine whether the regulation directly advances the governmental interest asserted, and whether it is not more extensive than is necessary to serve that interest." In this analysis, the Government bears the burden of identifying a substantial interest and justifying the challenged restriction.

The four parts of the *Central Hudson* test are not entirely discrete. All are important and, to a certain extent, interrelated: Each raises a relevant question that may not be dispositive to the First Amendment inquiry, but the answer to which may inform a judgment concerning the other three. Partly because of these intricacies, petitioners as well as certain judges, scholars, and *amici curiae* have advocated repudiation of the *Central Hudson* standard and implementation of a more straightforward and stringent test for assessing the validity of governmental restrictions on commercial speech. As the opinions in *44 Liquormart* demonstrate, reasonable judges may disagree about the merits of such proposals. It is, however, an established part of our constitutional jurisprudence that we do not ordinarily reach out to make novel or unnecessarily broad pronouncements on constitutional issues when a case can be fully resolved on a narrower ground. In this case, there is no need to break new ground. *Central Hudson*, as applied in our more recent commercial speech cases, provides an adequate basis for decision.

All parties to this case agree that the messages petitioners wish to broadcast constitute commercial speech, and that these broadcasts would satisfy the first part of the *Central Hudson* test: Their content is not misleading and concerns lawful activities, *i.e.*, private casino gambling in Louisiana and Mississippi. As well, the proposed commercial messages would convey information—whether taken favorably or unfavorably by the audience—about an activity that is the subject of intense public debate in many communities. In addition, petitioners' broadcasts presumably would disseminate accurate information as to the operation of market competitors, such as pay-out ratios, which can benefit listeners by informing their consumption choices and fostering price competition. Thus, even if the broadcasters' interest in conveying these messages is entirely pecuniary, the interests of, and benefit to, the audience may be broader. See *Virginia Bd. of Pharmacy v. Virginia Citizens Consumer Council, Inc.*, (1976); *Linmark Associates, Inc. v. Willingboro* (1977).

The second part of the *Central Hudson* test asks whether the asserted governmental interest served by the speech restriction is substantial. The Solicitor General identifies two such interests: (1) reducing the social costs associated with "gambling" or "casino gambling," and (2) assisting States that "restrict gambling" or "prohibit casino gambling" within their own borders. Underlying Congress' statutory scheme, the Solicitor General contends, is the judgment that gambling contributes to corruption and organized crime; underwrites bribery, narcotics trafficking, and other illegal conduct; imposes a regressive tax on the poor; and "offers a false but sometimes irresistible hope of financial advancement." Brief for Respondents 15–16. With respect to casino gambling, the Solicitor General states that many of the associated social costs stem from "pathological" or "compulsive" gambling by approximately 3 million Americans, whose behavior is primarily associated with "continuous play" games, such as slot machines. He also observes that compulsive gambling has grown along with the expansion of legalized gambling nationwide, leading to billions of dollars in economic costs; injury and loss to these gamblers as well as their families, communities, and government; and street, white-collar, and organized crime.

We can accept the characterization of these two interests as "substantial," but that conclusion is by no means self-evident. No one seriously doubts that the Federal Government may assert a legitimate and substantial interest in alleviating the societal ills recited above, or in assisting like-minded States to do the same. But in the judgment of both the Congress and many state legislatures, the social costs that support the suppression of gambling are offset, and sometimes outweighed, by countervailing policy considerations, primarily in the form of economic benefits. Despite its awareness of the potential social costs, Congress has not only sanctioned casino gambling for Indian tribes through tribal-state compacts, but has enacted other statutes that reflect approval of state legislation that authorizes a host of public and private gambling activities. That Congress has generally exempted state-run lotteries and casinos from federal gambling legislation reflects a decision to defer to, and even promote, differing gambling policies in different States. Whatever its character in 1934 when §1304 was adopted, the federal policy of discouraging gambling in general, and casino gambling in particular, is now decidedly equivocal.

Of course, it is not our function to weigh the policy arguments on either side of the nationwide debate over whether and to what extent casino and other forms of gambling should be legalized. Moreover, enacted congressional policy and "governmental interests" are not necessarily equivalents for purposes of commercial speech analysis. But we cannot ignore Congress' unwillingness to adopt a single national policy that consistently endorses either interest asserted by the Solicitor General. Even though the Government has identified substantial interests, when we consider both their quality and the information sought to be suppressed, the crosscurrents in the scope and application of §1304 become more difficult for the Government to defend.

The third part of the *Central Hudson* test asks whether the speech restriction directly and materially advances the asserted governmental interest. "This burden is not satisfied by mere speculation or conjecture; rather, a governmental body seeking to sustain a restriction on commercial speech must demonstrate that the harms it recites are real and that its restriction will in fact alleviate them to a material degree." Consequently, "the regulation may not be sustained if it provides only ineffective or remote support for the government's purpose." We have observed that "this requirement is critical; otherwise, 'a State could with ease restrict commercial speech in the service of other objectives that could not themselves justify a burden on commercial expression.'" The fourth part of the test complements the direct-advancement inquiry of the third, asking whether the speech restriction is not more extensive than necessary to serve the interests that support it. The Government is not required to employ the least restrictive means conceivable, but it must demonstrate narrow tailoring of the challenged regulation to the asserted interest—"a fit that is not necessarily perfect, but reasonable; that represents not necessarily the single best disposition but one whose scope is in proportion to the interest served." On the whole, then, the challenged regulation should indicate that its proponent "'carefully calculated' the costs and benefits associated with the burden on speech imposed by its prohibition."

As applied to petitioners' case, §1304 cannot satisfy these standards. With regard to the first asserted interest—alleviating the social costs of casino gambling by limiting demand—the Government contends that its broadcasting restrictions directly advance that interest because "promotional" broadcast advertising concerning casino gambling increases demand for such gambling, which in turn increases the amount of casino gambling that produces those social costs. Additionally, the Government believes that compulsive gamblers are especially susceptible to the pervasiveness and potency of broadcast advertising. Assuming the accuracy of this causal chain, it does not necessarily follow that the Government's speech ban has directly and materially furthered the asserted interest. While it is no doubt fair to assume that more advertising would have some impact on overall demand for gambling, it is also reasonable to assume that much of that advertising would merely channel gamblers to one casino rather than another. More important, any measure of the effectiveness of the Government's attempt to minimize the social costs of gambling cannot ignore Congress' simultaneous encouragement of tribal casino gambling, which may well be growing at a rate exceeding any increase in gambling or compulsive gambling that private casino advertising could produce. And, as the Court of Appeals recognized, the Government fails to "connect casino gambling and compulsive gambling with broadcast advertising for casinos"—let alone broadcast advertising for non-Indian commercial casinos.

We need not resolve the question whether any lack of evidence in the record fails to satisfy the standard of proof under *Central Hudson*, however, because the flaw in the Government's case is more fundamental: The operation of §1304 and its attendant regulatory regime is so pierced by exemptions and inconsistencies that the Government cannot hope to exonerate it. Under current law, a broadcaster may not carry advertising about privately operated commercial casino gambling, regardless of the location of the station or the casino. On the other hand, advertisements for tribal casino gambling authorized by state compacts—whether operated by the tribe or by a private party pursuant to a management contract—are subject to no such broadcast ban, even if the broadcaster is located in or broadcasts to a jurisdiction with the strictest of antigambling policies. Government-operated, nonprofit, and "occasional and ancillary" commercial casinos are likewise exempt.

The FCC's interpretation and application of §1304 underscore the statute's infirmity. Attempting to enforce the underlying purposes and policy of the statute, the FCC has permitted broadcasters to tempt viewers with claims of "Vegas-style excitement" at a commercial "casino," if "casino" is part of the establishment's proper name and the advertisement can be taken to refer to the casino's amenities, rather than directly promote its gaming aspects. While we can hardly fault the FCC in view of the statute's focus on the suppression of certain types of information, the agency's practice is squarely at odds with the governmental interests asserted in this case.

From what we can gather, the Government is committed to prohibiting accurate product information, not commercial enticements of all kinds, and then only when conveyed over certain forms of media and for certain types of gambling—indeed, for only certain brands of *casino* gambling—and despite the fact that messages about the availability of such gambling are being conveyed over the airwaves by other speakers.

Even putting aside the broadcast exemptions for arguably distinguishable sorts of gambling that might also give rise to social costs about which the Federal Government is concerned—such as state lotteries and pari-mutuel betting on horse and dog races—the Government presents no convincing reason for pegging its speech ban to the identity of the owners or operators of the advertised casinos. The Government cites revenue needs of States and tribes that conduct casino gambling, and notes that net revenues generated by the tribal casinos are dedicated to the welfare of the tribes and their members. Yet the Government admits that tribal casinos offer precisely the same types of gambling as private casinos. Further, the Solicitor General does not maintain that government-operated casino gaming is any different, that States cannot derive revenue from taxing private casinos, or that any one class of casino operators is likely to advertise in a meaningfully distinct manner than the others. The Government's suggestion that Indian casinos are too isolated to warrant attention is belied by a quick review of tribal geography and the Government's own evidence regarding the financial success of tribal gaming. If distance were determinative, Las Vegas might have remained a relatively small community, or simply disappeared like a desert mirage.

Ironically, the most significant difference identified by the Government between tribal and other classes of casino gambling is that the former are "heavily regulated." If such direct regulation provides a basis for believing that the social costs of gambling in tribal casinos are sufficiently mitigated to make their advertising tolerable, one would have thought that Congress might have at least experimented with comparable regulation before abridging the speech rights of federally *un*regulated casinos. While Congress' failure to institute such direct regulation of private casino gambling does not necessarily compromise the constitutionality of §1304, it does undermine the asserted justifications for the restriction before us. There surely are practical and nonspeech-related forms of regulation— including a prohibition or supervision of gambling on credit; limitations on the use of cash machines on casino premises; controls on admissions; pot or betting limits; location restrictions; and licensing requirements—that could more directly and effectively alleviate some of the social costs of casino gambling. . . .

Given the special federal interest in protecting the welfare of Native Americans, we recognize that there may be valid reasons for imposing commercial regulations on non-Indian businesses that differ from those imposed on tribal enterprises. It does not follow, however, that those differences also justify abridging non-Indians' freedom of speech more severely than the freedom of their tribal competitors. For the power to prohibit or to regulate particular conduct does not necessarily include the power to prohibit or regulate speech about that conduct. It is well settled that the First Amendment mandates closer scrutiny of government restrictions on speech than of its regulation of commerce alone. And to the extent that the purpose and operation of federal law distinguishes among information about tribal, governmental, and private casinos based on the identity of their owners or operators, the Government presents no sound reason why such lines bear any meaningful relationship to the particular interest asserted: minimizing casino gambling and its social costs by way of a (partial) broadcast ban. Even under the degree of scrutiny that we have applied in commercial speech cases, decisions that select among speakers conveying virtually identical messages are in serious tension with the principles undergirding the First Amendment. The second interest asserted by the Government—the derivative goal of "assisting" States with policies that disfavor private casinos—adds little to its case. We cannot see how this broadcast restraint, ambivalent as it is, might directly and adequately further any *state* interest in dampening consumer demand for casino gambling if it cannot achieve the same goal with respect to the similar *federal* interest. . . .

Accordingly, respondents cannot overcome the presumption that the speaker and the audience, not the Government, should be left to assess the value of accurate and nonmisleading information about lawful conduct. Had the Federal Government adopted a more coherent policy, or accommodated the rights of speakers in States that have legalized the underlying conduct, this might be a different case. But under current federal law, as applied to petitioners and the messages that they wish to convey, the broadcast prohibition in 18 U.S.C. §1304 (1998) violates the First Amendment. The judgment of the Court of Appeals is therefore

Reversed.

JUSTICE THOMAS, concurring in the judgment.

I continue to adhere to my view that "[i]n cases such as this, in which the government's asserted interest is to keep legal users of a product or service ignorant in order to manipulate their choices in the marketplace," the *Central Hudson* test should not be applied because "such an 'interest' is *per se* illegitimate and can no more justify regulation of 'commercial speech' than it can justify regulation of 'noncommercial' speech." *44 Liquormart, Inc. v. Rhode Island*, (1996) (concurring in part and concurring in the judgment). Accordingly, I concur only in the judgment.

CHAPTER 9

INVESTIGATIONS AND EVIDENCE

THE USE OF ILLEGALLY OBTAINED EVIDENCE

Since the establishment of the exclusionary rule in *Mapp v. Ohio* (1961), conservative-leaning members of the Court have attempted to narrow its application. The 1984 decisions in *United States v. Leon* and *Nix v. Williams* moved toward this goal by establishing certain exceptions to the rule's directive that evidence gathered illegally should be inadmissible at trial. *Pennsylvania Board of Probation and Parole v. Scott* (1998) continues the battle over the status of the exclusionary rule and its application. Once again, we see an ideologically divided Court split over whether unconstitutionally gathered evidence should be used in a judicial proceeding—in this case, a parole revocation hearing.

Pennsylvania Board of Probation and Parole v. Scott

_____ U.S. _____ (1998)

Vote: 5 (Kennedy, O'Connor, Rehnquist, Scalia, Thomas)
    4 (Breyer, Ginsburg, Souter, Stevens)
Opinion of the Court: Thomas
Dissenting Opinions: Stevens, Souter

Keith M. Scott pleaded no contest to a charge of third-degree murder and was sentenced to a prison term of ten to twenty years, beginning March 31, 1983. In September 1993, shortly after completing the minimum sentence, Scott was released on parole. Among the parole conditions to which Scott agreed was a prohibition against "owning or possessing any firearms or other weapons." He also consented to any future search by parole officials seeking evidence of parole violations.

Five months after Scott was released, parole officials obtained an arrest warrant based on evidence that he had violated several conditions of his parole, including the possession of weapons, the consumption of alcohol, and the assault of a co-worker. Scott was arrested at a local diner by three parole officers. Scott gave the officers the keys to his residence, a home owned by his mother. With the mother present, the officers searched Scott's bedroom, but found nothing related to the suspected offenses. In an adjacent sitting room, however, they found five firearms, a compound bow, and arrows. At no time did the officers obtain the permission of Scott's mother to conduct the search.

At his parole revocation hearing, Scott's lawyers objected to the introduction of the weapons on the grounds that the search of the mother's home without permission or warrant was unreasonable. The hearing examiner, however, rejected these arguments and admitted the evidence. As a result, Scott was found in violation of the parole conditions and sentenced to serve three years in prison. The Commonwealth Court of Pennsylvania overturned this ruling, holding that the search was illegal and that the seized evidence should have been excluded. This decision was affirmed by the Pennsylvania Supreme Court.

JUSTICE THOMAS delivered the opinion of the Court.

This case presents the question whether the exclusionary rule, which generally prohibits the introduction at criminal trial of evidence obtained in violation of a defendant's Fourth Amendment rights, applies in parole revocation hearings. We hold that it does not. . . .

We have emphasized repeatedly that the State's use of evidence obtained in violation of the Fourth Amendment does not itself violate the Constitution. See, e.g., *United States v. Leon* (1984); *Stone v. Powell* (1976). Rather, a Fourth Amendment violation is " 'fully accomplished' " by the illegal search or seizure, and no exclusion of evidence from a judicial or administrative proceeding can " 'cure the invasion of the defendant's rights which he has already suffered.' " *United States v. Leon.* The exclusionary rule is instead a judicially created means of deterring illegal searches and seizures. *United States v. Calandra* (1974). As such, the rule does not "proscribe the introduction of illegally seized evidence in all proceedings or against all persons," *Stone v. Powell,* but applies only in contexts "where its remedial objectives are thought most efficaciously served," *United States v. Calandra.* Moreover, because the rule is prudential rather than constitutionally mandated, we have held it to be applicable only where its deterrence benefits outweigh its "substantial social costs." *United States v. Leon.*

Recognizing these costs, we have repeatedly declined to extend the exclusionary rule to proceedings other than criminal trials. For example, in *United States v.*

Calandra, we held that the exclusionary rule does not apply to grand jury proceedings; in so doing, we emphasized that such proceedings play a special role in the law enforcement process and that the traditionally flexible, nonadversarial nature of those proceedings would be jeopardized by application of the rule. Likewise, in *United States v. Janis* [1976], we held that the exclusionary rule did not bar the introduction of unconstitutionally obtained evidence in a civil tax proceeding because the costs of excluding relevant and reliable evidence would outweigh the marginal deterrence benefits, which, we noted, would be minimal because the use of the exclusionary rule in criminal trials already deterred illegal searches. Finally, in *INS v. Lopez-Mendoza* (1984), we refused to extend the exclusionary rule to civil deportation proceedings, citing the high social costs of allowing an immigrant to remain illegally in this country and noting the incompatibility of the rule with the civil, administrative nature of those proceedings.

As in *Calandra, Janis,* and *Lopez-Mendoza,* we are asked to extend the operation of the exclusionary rule beyond the criminal trial context. We again decline to do so. Application of the exclusionary rule would both hinder the functioning of state parole systems and alter the traditionally flexible, administrative nature of parole revocation proceedings. The rule would provide only minimal deterrence benefits in this context, because application of the rule in the criminal trial context already provides significant deterrence of unconstitutional searches. We therefore hold that the federal exclusionary rule does not bar the introduction at parole revocation hearings of evidence seized in violation of parolees' Fourth Amendment rights.

Because the exclusionary rule precludes consideration of reliable, probative evidence, it imposes significant costs: it undeniably detracts from the truthfinding process and allows many who would otherwise be incarcerated to escape the consequences of their actions. Although we have held these costs to be worth bearing in certain circumstances, our cases have repeatedly emphasized that the rule's "costly toll" upon truth-seeking and law enforcement objectives presents a high obstacle for those urging application of the rule. *United States v. Payner* (1980).

The costs of excluding reliable, probative evidence are particularly high in the context of parole revocation proceedings. Parole is a "variation on imprisonment of convicted criminals," *Morrissey v. Brewer* (1972), in which the State accords a limited degree of freedom in return for the parolee's assurance that he will comply with the often strict terms and conditions of his release. In most cases, the State is willing to extend parole only because it is able to condition it upon compliance with certain requirements. The State thus has an "overwhelming interest" in ensuring that a parolee complies with those requirements and is returned to prison if he fails to do so. The exclusion of evidence establishing a parole violation, however, hampers the State's ability to ensure compliance with these conditions by permitting the parolee to avoid the consequences of his noncompliance. The costs of allowing a parolee to avoid the consequences of his violation are compounded by the fact that parolees (particularly those who have already committed parole violations) are more likely to commit future criminal offenses than are average citizens. Indeed, this is the very premise behind the system of close parole supervision.

The exclusionary rule, moreover, is incompatible with the traditionally flexible, administrative procedures of parole revocation. Because parole revocation deprives the parolee not "of the absolute liberty to which every citizen is entitled, but only of the conditional liberty properly dependent on observance of special parole restrictions," States have wide latitude under the Constitution to structure parole revocation proceedings. Most States, including Pennsylvania, have adopted informal, administrative parole revocation procedures in order to accommodate the large number of parole proceedings. These proceedings generally are not conducted by judges, but instead by parole boards, "members of which need not be judicial officers or lawyers." And traditional rules of evidence generally do not apply. Nor are these proceedings entirely adversarial, as they are designed to be " 'predictive and discretionary' as well as factfinding."

Application of the exclusionary rule would significantly alter this process. The exclusionary rule frequently requires extensive litigation to determine whether particular evidence must be excluded. Such litigation is inconsistent with the non-adversarial, administrative processes established by the States. Although States could adapt their parole revocation proceedings to accommodate such litigation, such a change would transform those proceedings from a "predictive and discretionary" effort to promote the best interests of both parolees and society into trial-like proceedings "less attuned" to the interests of the parolee. We are simply unwilling so to intrude into the States' correctional schemes. . . .

The deterrence benefits of the exclusionary rule would not outweigh these costs. As the Supreme Court of Pennsylvania recognized, application of the exclusionary rule to parole revocation proceedings would have little deterrent effect upon an officer who is unaware that the subject of his search is a parolee. In that situation, the officer will likely be searching for evidence of criminal conduct with an eye toward the introduction of the evidence at a criminal trial. The likelihood that illegally obtained evidence will be excluded from trial provides deterrence against Fourth Amendment violations, and the remote possibility that the subject is a parolee and that the evidence may be admitted at a parole revocation proceeding surely has little, if any, effect on the officer's incentives. . . .

We have long been averse to imposing federal requirements upon the parole systems of the States. A federal requirement that parole boards apply the exclusionary rule, which is itself a "but grudgingly taken medicament," *United States v. Janis* (1976), would severely disrupt the traditionally informal, administrative process of parole revocation. The marginal deterrence of unreasonable searches and seizures is insufficient to justify such an intrusion. We therefore hold that parole boards are not required by federal law to exclude evidence obtained in violation of the Fourth Amendment. Accordingly, the judgment below is reversed, and the case is remanded to the Pennsylvania Supreme Court.

It is so ordered.

JUSTICE SOUTER, with whom JUSTICE GINSBURG and JUSTICE BREYER join, dissenting.

The Court's holding that the exclusionary rule of *Mapp v. Ohio* (1961), has no application to parole revocation proceedings rests upon mistaken conceptions of the actual function of revocation, of the objectives of those who gather evidence in support of petitions to revoke, and, consequently, of the need to deter violations of the Fourth Amendment that would tend to occur in administering the parole laws. In reality a revocation proceeding often serves the same function as a criminal trial, and the revocation hearing may very well present the only forum in which the State will seek to use evidence of a parole violation, even when that evidence would support an independent criminal charge. The deterrent function of the exclusionary rule is therefore implicated as much by a revocation proceeding as by a conventional trial, and the exclusionary rule should be applied accordingly. From the Court's conclusion to the contrary, I respectfully dissent. . . .

. . . [T]he majority does not see that in the investigation of criminal conduct by someone known to be on parole, Fourth Amendment standards will have very little deterrent sanction unless evidence offered for parole revocation is subject to suppression for unconstitutional conduct. It is not merely that parole revocation is the government's consolation prize when, for whatever reason, it cannot obtain a further criminal conviction, though that will sometimes be true. What is at least equally telling is that parole revocation will frequently be pursued instead of prosecution as the course of choice, a fact recognized a quarter of a century ago when we observed in *Morrissey v. Brewer* [1972] that a parole revocation proceeding "is often preferred to a new prosecution because of the procedural ease of recommitting the individual on the basis of a lesser showing by the State."

The reasons for this tendency to skip any new prosecution are obvious. If the conduct in question is a crime in its own right, the odds of revocation are very high. Since time on the street before revocation is not subtracted from the balance of the sentence to be served on revocation, the balance may well be long enough to render recommitment the practical equivalent of a new sentence for a separate crime. And all of this may be accomplished without shouldering the burden of proof beyond a reasonable doubt; hence the obvious popularity of revocation in place of new prosecution.

The upshot is that without a suppression remedy in revocation proceedings, there will often be no influence capable of deterring Fourth Amendment violations when parole revocation is a possible response to new crime. Suppression in the revocation proceeding cannot be looked upon, then, as furnishing merely incremental or marginal deterrence over and above the effect of exclusion in criminal prosecution. Instead, it will commonly provide the only deterrence to unconstitutional conduct when the incarceration of parolees is sought, and the reasons that support the suppression remedy in prosecution therefore support it in parole revocation. . . .

Because the search violated the Fourth Amendment, and because I conclude that the exclusionary rule ought to apply to parole revocation proceedings, I would affirm the decision of the Supreme Court of Pennsylvania.

RESTRICTING GANG ACTIVITY

Crime is a problem with which all cities must deal. Chicago attempted to do so by prohibiting "criminal street gang members" from loitering with one another or with other persons in any public place.

Chicago surely viewed its ordinance as providing a service to the public. Because of gang presence many "residents of the inner city felt that they were prisoners in their own homes." But, at the same time, it raised grave questions concerning restrictions that governments may place on the personal liberty of their citizens.

How would the Court sort through these issues? *City of Chicago v. Morales* (1999) provides the answer, though one that provoked bitter dissents from several Court members.

City of Chicago v. Morales

_____ U.S. _____ (1999)

Vote: 6 (Breyer, Ginsburg, Kennedy, O'Connor, Souter, Stevens)
         3 (Rehnquist, Scalia, Thomas)
Opinion of the Court and Opinion Announcing the Judgment of the Court: Stevens
Concurring Opinions: Breyer, Kennedy, O'Connor
Dissenting Opinions: Thomas, Scalia

In an effort to deal with its escalating crime rate, which it largely attributed to street gang activity, the Chicago City Council adopted the Gang Congregation Ordinance in 1992. The ordinance makes it a crime for "criminal street gang members" to be "loitering" with one another or with other persons in any public place. To be charged with a violation of the act, (1) the police officer must reasonably believe that at least one of the two or more persons present in a "public place" is a "criminal street gang membe[r]"; (2) the persons must be "loitering," which the ordinance defines as "remain[ing] in any one place with no apparent purpose"; (3) the officer must then order "all" of the persons to disperse and remove themselves "from the area"; and (4) a person must disobey the officer's order. If any person, whether a gang member or not, disobeys the officer's order, that person is guilty of violating the ordinance and can receive a fine of up to $500, imprisonment for not more than six months, and a requirement to perform up to 120 hours of public service.

Two months after the ordinance was adopted the Chicago Police Department promulgated General Order 92–4 to provide guidelines to govern its enforcement. That order was designed to "to ensure that the anti–gang loitering ordinance is not enforced in an arbitrary or discriminatory way." It establishes detailed criteria for defining street gangs and membership in such gangs and it directs police commanders to "designate areas in which the presence of gang members has a demonstrable effect on the activities of law abiding persons in the surrounding community," as well as providing that the ordinance "will be enforced only within the designated areas." The city, however, does not make public the locations of these "designated areas."

Between 1992 and 1995, while the ordinance was in effect, the police issued over 89,000 dispersal orders and arrested over 42,000 people for violating it (including Jesus Morales). But the ordinance itself did not fare well in various court challenges. While two trial judges upheld its constitutionality, eleven others ruled that it was invalid.

The Illinois Supreme Court agreed with the majority of trial courts. It held that "the gang loitering ordinance violates due process of law in that it is impermissibly vague on its face and an arbitrary restriction on personal liberties." To support this conclusion, the court pointed out that the definition of "loitering" in the ordinance drew no distinction between innocent conduct and conduct calculated to cause harm. "Moreover, the definition of 'loiter' provided by the ordinance does not assist in clearly articulating the proscriptions of the ordinance."

After this decision, the city took the case to the U.S. Supreme Court. The Clinton administration, along with thirty-one states, filed briefs supporting the ordinance.

JUSTICE STEVENS delivered the opinion of the Court.

The basic factual predicate for the city's ordinance is not in dispute. As the city argues in its brief, "the very presence of a large collection of obviously brazen, insistent, and lawless gang members and hangers-on on the public ways intimidates residents, who become afraid even to leave their homes and go about their business. That, in turn, imperils community residents' sense of safety and security, detracts from property values, and can ultimately destabilize entire neighborhoods." The findings in the ordinance explain that it was motivated by these concerns. We have no doubt that a law that directly prohibited such intimidating conduct would be constitutional, but this ordinance broadly covers a significant amount of additional activity. Uncertainty about the scope of that additional coverage provides the basis for respondents' claim that the ordinance is too vague.

We are confronted at the outset with the city's claim that it was improper for the state courts to conclude that the ordinance is invalid on its face. The city correctly points out that imprecise laws can be attacked on their face under two different doctrines. First, the overbreadth doctrine permits the facial invalidation of laws that inhibit the exercise of First Amendment rights if the impermissible applications of the law are substantial when "judged in relation to the statute's plainly legitimate sweep." Second, even if an enactment does not reach a substantial amount of constitutionally protected conduct, it may be impermissibly vague because it fails to establish standards for the police and public that are sufficient to guard against the arbitrary deprivation of liberty interests. *Kolender v. Lawson* (1983).

While we, like the Illinois courts, conclude that the ordinance is invalid on its face, we do not rely on the overbreadth doctrine. We agree with the city's submission that the law does not have a sufficiently substantial impact on conduct protected by the First Amendment to render it unconstitutional. The ordinance does not prohibit speech. Because the term "loiter" is defined as remaining in one place "with no apparent purpose," it is also clear that it does not prohibit any form of conduct that is apparently intended to convey a message. By its terms, the ordinance is inapplicable to assemblies that are designed to demonstrate a group's support of, or opposition to, a particular point of view. On the other hand, as the United States recognizes, the freedom to loiter for innocent purposes is part of the "liberty" protected by the Due Process Clause of the Fourteenth Amendment. We have expressly identified this "right to remove from one place to another according to inclination" as "an attribute of personal liberty" protected by the Constitution. Indeed, it is apparent that an individual's decision to remain in a public place of his choice is as much a part of his liberty as the freedom of movement inside frontiers that is "a part of our heritage."

There is no need, however, to decide whether the impact of the Chicago ordinance on constitutionally protected liberty alone would suffice to support a facial challenge under the overbreadth doctrine. For it is clear that the vagueness of this enactment makes a facial challenge appropriate. This is not an ordinance that "simply regulates business behavior and contains a scienter requirement." It is a criminal law that contains no *mens rea* requirement, and infringes on constitutionally protected rights. When vagueness permeates the text of such a law, it is subject to facial attack.

Vagueness may invalidate a criminal law for either of two independent reasons. First, it may fail to provide the kind of notice that will enable ordinary people to understand what conduct it prohibits; second, it may authorize and even encourage arbitrary and discriminatory enforcement. Accordingly, we first consider whether the ordinance provides fair notice to the citizen and then discuss its potential for arbitrary enforcement.

"It is established that a law fails to meet the requirements of the Due Process Clause if it is so vague and standardless that it leaves the public uncertain as to the conduct it prohibits. . . ." The Illinois Supreme Court recognized that the term "loiter" may have a common and accepted meaning, but the definition of that term in this ordinance—"to remain in any one place with no apparent purpose"—does not. It is difficult to imagine how any citizen of the city of Chicago standing in a public place with a group of people would know if he or she had an "apparent purpose." If she were talking to another person, would she have an apparent purpose? If she were frequently checking her watch and looking expectantly down the street, would she have an apparent purpose? Since the city cannot conceivably have meant to criminalize each instance a citizen stands in public with a gang member, the vagueness that dooms this ordinance is not the product of uncertainty about the normal meaning of "loitering," but rather about what loitering is covered by the ordinance and what is not. The Illinois Supreme Court emphasized the law's failure to distinguish between innocent conduct and conduct threatening harm. Its decision followed the precedent set by a number of state courts that have upheld ordinances that criminalize loitering combined with some other overt act or evidence of criminal intent. However, state courts have uniformly invalidated laws that do not join the term "loitering" with a second specific element of the crime. The city's principal response to this concern about adequate notice is that loiterers are not subject to sanction until after they have failed to comply with an officer's order to disperse. "[W]hatever problem is created by a law that criminalizes conduct people normally believe to be innocent is solved when persons receive actual notice from a police order of what they are expected to do." We find this response unpersuasive for at least two reasons.

First, the purpose of the fair notice requirement is to enable the ordinary citizen to conform his or her conduct to the law. Although it is true that a loiterer is not subject to criminal sanctions unless he or she disobeys a dispersal order, the loitering is the conduct that the ordinance is designed to prohibit. If the loitering is in fact harmless and innocent, the dispersal order itself is an unjustified impairment of liberty. If the police are able to decide arbitrarily which members of the public they will order to disperse, then the Chicago ordinance becomes indistinguishable from the law we held invalid in *Shuttlesworth v. Birmingham* (1965). Because an officer may issue an order only after prohibited conduct has already occurred, it cannot provide the kind of advance notice that will protect the putative loiterer from being ordered to disperse. Such an order cannot retroactively give adequate warning of the boundary between the permissible and the impermissible applications of the law.

Second, the terms of the dispersal order compound the inadequacy of the notice afforded by the ordinance. It provides that the officer "shall order all such persons to disperse and remove themselves from the area." This vague phrasing raises a host of questions. After such an order issues, how long must the loiterers remain apart? How far must they move? If each loiterer walks around the block and they meet again at the same location, are they subject to arrest or merely to being ordered to disperse again? As we do here, we have found vagueness in a criminal statute exacerbated by the use of the standards of "neighborhood" and "locality."

Lack of clarity in the description of the loiterer's duty to obey a dispersal order might not render the ordinance unconstitutionally vague if the definition of the forbidden conduct were clear, but it does buttress our conclusion that the entire ordinance fails to give the ordinary citizen adequate notice of what is forbidden and what is permitted. The Constitution does not permit a legislature to "set a net large enough to catch all possible offenders, and leave it to the courts to step inside and say who could be rightfully detained, and who should be set at large." This ordinance is therefore vague "not in the sense that it requires a person to conform his conduct to an imprecise but comprehensible normative standard, but rather in the sense that no standard of conduct is specified at all."

The broad sweep of the ordinance also violates "'the requirement that a legislature establish minimal guidelines to govern law enforcement.'" There are no such guidelines in the ordinance. In any public place in the city of Chicago, persons who stand or sit in the company of a gang member may be ordered to disperse unless their purpose is apparent. The mandatory language in the enactment directs the police to issue an order without first making any inquiry about their possible purposes. It matters not whether the reason that a gang member and his father, for example, might loiter near Wrigley Field is to rob an unsuspecting fan or just to get a glimpse of Sammy Sosa leaving the ballpark; in either event, if their purpose is not apparent to a nearby police officer, she may—indeed, she "shall—order them to disperse.". . .

Presumably an officer would have discretion to treat some purposes—perhaps a purpose to engage in idle conversation or simply to enjoy a cool breeze on a warm evening—as too frivolous to be apparent if he suspected a different ulterior motive. Moreover, an officer conscious of the city council's reasons for enacting the ordinance might well ignore its text and issue a dispersal order, even though an illicit purpose is actually apparent.

It is true, as the city argues, that the requirement that the officer reasonably believe that a group of loiterers contains a gang member does place a limit on the authority to order dispersal. That limitation would no doubt be sufficient if the ordinance only applied to loitering that had an apparently harmful purpose or effect, or possibly if it only applied to loitering by persons reasonably believed to be criminal gang members. But this ordinance, for reasons that are not explained in the findings of the city council, requires no harmful purpose and applies to non-gang members as well as suspected gang members. It applies to everyone in the city who may remain in one place with one suspected gang member as long as their purpose is not apparent to an officer observing them. Friends, relatives, teachers, counselors, or even total strangers might unwittingly engage in forbidden loitering if they happen to engage in idle conversation with a gang member.

Ironically, the definition of loitering in the Chicago ordinance not only extends its scope to encompass harmless conduct, but also has the perverse consequence of excluding from its coverage much of the intimidating conduct that motivated its enactment. As the city council's findings demonstrate, the most harmful gang loitering is motivated either by an apparent purpose to publicize the gang's dominance of certain territory, thereby intimidating nonmembers, or by an equally apparent purpose to conceal ongoing commerce in illegal drugs. As the Illinois Supreme Court has not placed any limiting construction on the language in the ordinance, we must assume that the ordinance means what it says and that it has no application to loiterers whose purpose is apparent. The relative importance of its application to harmless loitering is magnified by its inapplicability to loitering that has an obviously threatening or illicit purpose. . . .

We recognize the serious and difficult problems testified to by the citizens of Chicago that led to the enactment of this ordinance. "We are mindful that the preservation of liberty depends in part on the maintenance of social order. However, in this instance the city has enacted an ordinance that affords too much discretion to the police and too little notice to citizens who wish to use the public streets.

Accordingly, the judgment of the Supreme Court of Illinois is

Affirmed.

JUSTICE O'CONNOR, with whom JUSTICE BREYER joins, concurring in part and concurring in the judgment.

It is important to courts and legislatures alike that we characterize more clearly the narrow scope of today's holding. As the ordinance comes to this Court, it is unconstitutionally vague. Nevertheless, there remain open to Chicago reasonable alternatives to combat the very real threat posed by gang intimidation and violence. For example, the Court properly and expressly distinguishes the ordinance from laws that require loiterers to have a "harmful purpose," see *id.,* at 18, from laws that target only gang members, and from laws that incorporate limits on the area and manner in which the laws may be enforced. In addition, the ordinance here is unlike a law that "directly prohibit[s]" the "'presence of a large collection of obviously brazen, insistent, and lawless gang members and hangers-on on the public ways," that "'intimidates residents.'" Indeed, as the plurality notes, the city of Chicago has several laws that do exactly this. Chicago has even enacted a provision that "enables police officers to fulfill . . . traditional functions," including "preserving the public peace." Specifically, Chicago's general disorderly conduct provision allows the police to arrest those who knowingly "provoke, make or aid in making a breach of peace." In my view, the gang loitering ordinance could have been construed more narrowly. The term "loiter" might possibly be construed in a more limited fashion to mean "to remain in any one place with no apparent purpose other than to establish control over identifiable areas, to intimidate others from entering those areas, or to conceal illegal activities." Such a definition would be consistent with the Chicago City Council's findings and would avoid the vagueness problems of the ordinance as construed by the Illinois Supreme Court. As noted above, so would limitations that restricted the ordinance's criminal penalties to gang members or that more carefully delineated the circumstances in which those penalties would apply to nongang members.

JUSTICE KENNEDY, concurring in part and concurring in the judgment.
As interpreted by the Illinois Supreme Court, the Chicago ordinance would

reach a broad range of innocent conduct. For this reason it is not necessarily saved by the requirement that the citizen must disobey a police order to disperse before there is a violation. We have not often examined these types of orders. It can be assumed, however, that some police commands will subject a citizen to prosecution for disobeying whether or not the citizen knows why the order is given. Illustrative examples include when the police tell a pedestrian not to enter a building and the reason is to avoid impeding a rescue team, or to protect a crime scene, or to secure an area for the protection of a public official. It does not follow, however, that any unexplained police order must be obeyed without notice of the lawfulness of the order. The predicate of an order to disperse is not, in my view, sufficient to eliminate doubts regarding the adequacy of notice under this ordinance. A citizen, while engaging in a wide array of innocent conduct, is not likely to know when he may be subject to a dispersal order based on the officer's own knowledge of the identity or affiliations of other persons with whom the citizen is congregating; nor may the citizen be able to assess what an officer might conceive to be the citizen's lack of an apparent purpose.

JUSTICE BREYER, concurring in part and concurring in the judgment.

The ordinance before us creates more than a "*minor* limitation upon the free state of nature." (Scalia, J., dissenting) (emphasis added). The law authorizes a police officer to order any person to remove himself from any "location open to the public, whether publicly or privately owned," *i.e.*, any sidewalk, front stoop, public park, public square, lakeside promenade, hotel, restaurant, bowling alley, bar, barbershop, sports arena, shopping mall, etc., but with two, and only two, limitations: First, that person must be accompanied by (or must himself be) someone police reasonably believe is a gang member. Second, that person must have remained in that public place "with no apparent purpose." The first limitation cannot save the ordinance. Though it limits the number of persons subject to the law, it leaves many individuals, gang members and nongang members alike, subject to its strictures. Nor does it limit in any way the range of conduct that police may prohibit. The second limitation is, not a limitation at all. Since one always has some apparent purpose, the so-called limitation invites, in fact requires, the policeman to interpret the words "no apparent purpose" as meaning "no apparent purpose except for . . . ." And it is in the ordinance's delegation to the policeman of open-ended discretion to fill in that blank that the problem lies. To grant to a policeman virtually standardless discretion to close off major portions of the city to an innocent person is, in my view, to create a major, not a "minor," "limitation upon the free state of nature."

Nor does it violate "our rules governing facia challenges," (Scalia, J., dissenting), to forbid the city to apply the unconstitutional ordinance in this case. The reason *why* the ordinance is invalid explains how that is so. As I have said, I believe the ordinance violates the Constitution because it delegates too much discretion to a police officer to decide whom to order to move on, and in what circumstances.

And I see no way to distinguish in the ordinance's terms between one application of that discretion and another. The ordinance is unconstitutional, not because a policeman applied this discretion wisely or poorly in a particular case, but rather because the policeman enjoys too much discretion in *every* case. And if every application of the ordinance represents an exercise of unlimited discretion, then the ordinance *is* invalid in all its applications. The city of Chicago may be able validly to apply some *other* law to the defendants in light of their conduct. But the city of Chicago may no more apply *this* law to the defendants, no matter how they behaved, than could it apply an (imaginary) statute that said, "It is a crime to do wrong," even to the worst of murderers. Justice Scalia's examples reach a different conclusion because they assume a different basis for the law's constitutional invalidity. A statute, for example, might not provide fair warning to many, but an individual defendant might still have been aware that it prohibited the conduct in which he engaged. But I believe this ordinance is unconstitutional, not because it provides insufficient notice, but because it does not provide "sufficient minimal standards to guide law enforcement officers." . . .

JUSTICE SCALIA, dissenting.

Until the ordinance that is before us today was adopted, the citizens of Chicago were free to stand about in public places with no apparent purpose—to engage, that is, in conduct that appeared to be loitering. In recent years, however, the city has been afflicted with criminal street gangs. As reflected in the record before us, these gangs congregated in public places to deal in drugs, and to terrorize the neighborhoods by demonstrating control over their "turf." Many residents of the inner city felt that they were prisoners in their own homes. Once again, Chicagoans decided that to eliminate the problem it was worth restricting some of the freedom that they once enjoyed. The means they took was similar to the second, and more mild, example given above rather than the first: Loitering was not made unlawful, but when a group of people occupied a public place without an apparent purpose and in the company of a known gang member, police officers were authorized to order them to disperse, and the failure to obey such an order was made unlawful. See Chicago Municipal Code §8–4–015 (1992). The minor limitation upon the free state of nature that this prophylactic arrangement imposed upon all Chicagoans seemed to them (and it seems to me) a small price to pay for liberation of their streets.

The majority today invalidates this perfectly reasonable measure by ignoring our rules governing facial challenges, by elevating loitering to a constitutionally guaranteed right, and by discerning vagueness where, according to our usual standards, none exists . . . .

When our normal criteria for facial challenges are applied, it is clear that the Justices in the majority have transposed the burden of proof. Instead of requiring the respondents, who are challenging the Ordinance, to show that it is invalid in all its applications, they have required the petitioner to show that it is valid in all its applications. Both the plurality opinion and the concurrences display a lively imagination, creating hypothetical situations in which the law's application would (in their view) be ambiguous. But that creative role has been usurped from the petitioner, who can defeat the respondents' facial challenge by conjuring up a *single valid application* of the law. My contribution would go something like this: Tony, a member of the Jets criminal street gang, is standing alongside and chatting with fellow gang members while staking out their turf at Promontory Point on the South Side of Chicago; the group is flashing gang signs and displaying their distinctive tattoos to passersby. Officer Krupke, applying the Ordinance at issue here, orders the group to disperse. After some speculative discussion (probably irrelevant here) over whether the Jets are depraved because they are deprived, Tony and the other gang members break off further conversation with the statement— not entirely coherent, but evidently intended to be rude—"Gee, Officer Krupke, krup you." A tense standoff ensues until Officer Krupke arrests the group for failing to obey his dispersal order. Even assuming (as the Justices in the majority do, but I do not) that a law requiring obedience to a dispersal order is impermissibly vague unless it is clear to the objects of the order, before its issuance, that their conduct justifies it, I find it hard to believe that the Jets would not have known they had it coming. That should settle the matter of respondents' facial challenge to the Ordinance's vagueness. . . .

The plurality's explanation for its departure from the usual rule governing facial challenges is seemingly contained in the following statement: "[This] is a criminal law that contains no *mens rea* requirement . . . *and* infringes on constitutionally protected rights. . . . When vagueness permeates the text of *such* a law, it is subject to facial attack." The proposition is set forth with such assurance that one might suppose that it repeats some well-accepted formula in our jurisprudence: (Criminal law without *mens rea* requirement) + (infringement of constitutionally protected right) + (vagueness) = (entitlement to facial invalidation). There is no such formula; the plurality has made it up for this case, as the absence of any citation demonstrates.

But no matter. None of the three factors that the plurality relies upon exists anyway. I turn first to the support for the proposition that there is a constitutionally protected right to loiter—nor, as the plurality more favorably describes it, for a person to "remain in a public place of his choice." The plurality thinks much of this Fundamental Freedom to Loiter, which it contrasts with such lesser, constitutionally *un*protected, activities as doing (ugh!) *business*: "This is not an ordinance that simply regulates business behavior and contains a scienter requirement. . . . It is a criminal law that contains no *mens rea* requirement . . . and infringes on constitutionally protected rights." *Ibid.* (internal quotation marks omitted). (Poor Alexander Hamilton, who has seen his "commercial republic" devolve, in the eyes of the plurality, at least, into an "indolent republic," see The Federalist No. 6, p. 56; No. 11, pp. 84–91 (C. Rossiter ed. 1961).)

Of course every activity, even scratching one's head, can be called a "constitutional right" if one means by that term nothing more than the fact that the activity is covered (as all are) by the Equal Protection Clause, so that those who engage in it cannot be singled out without "rational basis." But using the term in that sense utterly impoverishes our constitutional discourse. We would then need a new term for those activities—such as political speech or religious worship—that cannot be forbidden even *with* rational basis.

The plurality tosses around the term "constitutional right" in this renegade sense, because there is not the slightest evidence for the existence of a genuine constitutional right to loiter. Justice Thomas recounts the vast historical tradition of criminalizing the activity. It is simply not maintainable that the right to loiter would have been regarded as an essential attribute of liberty at the time of the framing or at the time of adoption of the Fourteenth Amendment. For the plurality, however, the historical practices of our people are nothing more than a speed bump on the road to the "right" result. . . .

I turn next to that element of the plurality's facial-challenge formula which consists of the proposition that this criminal ordinance contains no *mens rea* requirement. The first step in analyzing this proposition is to determine what the *actus reus*, to which that *mens rea* is supposed to be attached, consists of. The majority believes that loitering forms part of (indeed, the essence of) the offense, and must be proved if conviction is to be obtained. That is not what the Ordinance provides. The only part of the Ordinance that refers to loitering is the portion that addresses, not the punishable conduct of the defendant, but what the police officer must observe before he can issue an order to disperse; and what he must observe is carefully defined in terms of what the defendant *appears* to be doing, not in terms of what the defendant is *actually* doing. The Ordinance does not require that the defendant have been loitering (*i.e.*, have been remaining in one place with no purpose), but rather that the police officer have observed him remaining in one place without any *apparent* purpose. Someone who in fact *has* a genuine purpose for remaining where he is (waiting for a friend, for example, or waiting to hold up a bank) *can* be ordered to move on (assuming the other conditions of the Ordinance are met), so long as his remaining has no *apparent* purpose. It is likely, to be sure, that the Ordinance will come down most heavily upon those who are *actually* loitering (those who *really* have no purpose in remaining where they are); but that activity is not a condition for issuance of the dispersal order.

The *only* act of a defendant that is made punishable by the Ordinance—or, indeed, that is even mentioned by the Ordinance—is his failure to "promptly obey" an order to disperse. The question, then, is whether that *actus reus* must be accompanied by any wrongful intent—and of course it must. As the Court itself describes the requirement, "a person must *disobey* the officer's order." *Ante*, at 3 (emphasis added). No one thinks a defendant could be successfully prosecuted under the Ordinance if he did not hear the order to disperse, or if he suffered a paralysis that rendered his compliance impossible. The willful failure to obey a police order is wrongful intent enough.

Finally, I address the last of the three factors in the plurality's facial-challenge formula: the proposition that the Ordinance is vague. It is not. Even under the ersatz overbreadth standard applied in *Kolender v. Lawson* (1983), which allows facial challenges if a law reaches "a substantial amount of constitutionally protected conduct," respondents' claim fails because the Ordinance would not be vague in most or even a substantial number of applications. A law is unconstitutionally vague if its lack of definitive standards either (1) fails to apprise persons of ordinary intelligence of the prohibited conduct, or (2) encourages arbitrary and discriminatory enforcement. The plurality relies primarily upon the first of these aspects. Since, it reasons, "the loitering is the conduct that the ordinance is designed to prohibit," and "an officer may issue an order only after prohibited conduct has already occurred," the order to disperse cannot itself serve "to apprise persons of ordinary intelligence of the prohibited conduct." What counts for purposes of vagueness analysis, however, is not what the Ordinance is "designed to prohibit," but what it actually subjects to criminal penalty. As discussed earlier, that consists of nothing but the refusal to obey a dispersal order, as to which there is no doubt of adequate notice of the prohibited conduct. The plurality's suggestion that even the dispersal order *itself* is unconstitutionally vague, because it does not specify *how far to disperse* (!) , scarcely requires a response. If it were true, it would render unconstitutional for vagueness many of the Presidential proclamations issued under that provision of the United States Code which requires the President, before using the militia or the Armed Forces for law enforcement, to issue a proclamation ordering the insurgents to disperse. President Eisenhower's proclamation relating to the obstruction of court-ordered enrollment of black students in public schools at Little Rock, Arkansas, read as follows: "I . . . command all persons engaged in such obstruction of justice to cease and desist therefrom, and to disperse forthwith." . . . The citizens of Chicago have decided that depriving themselves of the freedom to "hang out" with a gang member is necessary to eliminate pervasive gang crime and intimidation—and that the elimination of the one is worth the deprivation of the other. This Court has no business second-guessing either the degree of necessity or the fairness of the trade.

I dissent from the judgment of the Court.

JUSTICE THOMAS, with whom the CHIEF JUSTICE and JUSTICE SCALIA join, dissenting.

As part of its ongoing effort to curb the deleterious effects of criminal street gangs, the citizens of Chicago sensibly decided to return to basics. The ordinance does nothing more than confirm the well-established principle that the police have the duty and the power to maintain the public peace, and, when necessary, to disperse groups of individuals who threaten it. The plurality, however, concludes that the city's commonsense effort to combat gang loitering fails constitutional scrutiny for two separate reasons—because it infringes upon gang members' constitutional right to "loiter for innocent purposes," and because it is vague on its face. A majority of the Court endorses the latter conclusion. I respectfully disagree.

The plurality's sweeping conclusion that this ordinance infringes upon a liberty interest protected by the Fourteenth Amendment's Due Process Clause withers when exposed to the relevant history: Laws prohibiting loitering and vagrancy have been a fixture of Anglo-American law at least since the time of the Norman

Conquest. The American colonists enacted laws modeled upon the English vagrancy laws, and at the time of the founding, state and local governments customarily criminalized loitering and other forms of vagrancy. Vagrancy laws were common in the decades preceding the ratification of the Fourteenth Amendment, and remained on the books long after.

Tellingly, the plurality cites only three cases in support of the asserted right to "loiter for innocent purposes." Of those, only one—decided more than 100 years after the ratification of the Fourteenth Amendment—actually addressed the validity of a vagrancy ordinance. That case, *Papachristou* , contains some dicta that can be read to support the fundamental right that the plurality asserts. However, the Court in *Papachristou* did not undertake the now-accepted analysis applied in substantive due process cases—it did not look to tradition to define the rights protected by the Due Process Clause. In any event, a careful reading of the opinion reveals that the Court never said anything about a constitutional right. Today, the Court focuses extensively on the "rights" of gang members and their companions. It can safely do so—the people who will have to live with the consequences of today's opinion do not live in our neighborhoods. Rather, the people who will suffer from our lofty pronouncements are people like Ms. Susan Mary Jackson; people who have seen their neighborhoods literally destroyed by gangs and violence and drugs. They are good, decent people who must struggle to overcome their desperate situation, against all odds, in order to raise their families, earn a living, and remain good citizens. As one resident described, "There is only about maybe one or two percent of the people in the city causing these problems maybe, but it's keeping 98 percent of us in our houses and off the streets and afraid to shop." By focusing exclusively on the imagined "rights" of the two percent, the Court today has denied our most vulnerable citizens the very thing that Justice Stevens, *ante*, at 10, elevates above all else—the "freedom of movement." And that is a shame. I respectfully dissent.

THE PRESS AND CRIMINAL INVESTIGATIONS

Beginning in the 1960s and continuing through the 1980s the Court considered several cases centering on this question: How can judges keep trials fair without interfering with the rights of the press and the public?

Wilson v. Lane also involves the media's interest in reporting about crime—but here the issue is not about the balance between the freedom of the press and the right to a fair trial. Rather, the Court addressed the question whether, under the Fourth Amendment, police may invite representatives of the media to accompany them (a so-called "media ride-along") when they are executing a warrant.

How did the Court respond to this question? Is its answer in line with those it has offered in the fair trial cases?

Wilson v. Lane

_____ U.S. _____ (1999)

Vote: 9 (Breyer, Ginsburg, Kennedy, O'Connor, Rehnquist, Scalia, Souter, Stevens, Thomas)
0

Opinion of the Court: Rehnquist
Opinion Concurring in Part and Dissenting in Part: Stevens

In April 1992 police obtained three warrants for the arrest of Dominic Wilson, who had violated his probation on previous felony charges of robbery, theft, and assault with intent to rob. The police computer listed "caution indicators" that he was likely to be armed, resist arrest, and "assaul[t] police"; it also listed his address as 909 North Stone Street Avenue in Rockville, Maryland. Unknown to the police, this was actually the home of Wilson's parents.

When authorities went to execute the warrant in the early morning hours of April 16, 1992, they invited a reporter and a photographer from the *Washington Post* to accompany them. With these media representatives in tow, they entered the North Stone Street Avenue house, where Charles and Geraldine Wilson were still in bed. Assuming Charles Wilson was Dominic, the officers restrained him. It was only after they conducted a protective sweep of the house that the officers learned that Dominic Wilson was not there, and they departed. During the time that the officers were in the house, the *Washington Post* photographer took numerous pictures. The print reporter was also apparently in the living room observing the interaction between the police and Charles Wilson. At no time, however, were the reporters involved in the execution of the arrest warrant. And the *Washington Post* never published its photographs of the incident.

Charles and Geraldine Wilson brought suit against the law enforcement officials in their personal capacities for money. They contended that the officers' actions in bringing members of the media to observe and record the attempted execution of the arrest warrant violated their Fourth Amendment rights.

The Supreme Court dealt with two questions in its decision: (1) whether, under the Fourth Amendment, police may invite representatives of the media to accompany them (a so-called "media ride-along") when they are executing a warrant, and (2) whether the officers could be sued. All but Justice John Paul Stevens answered the second question in the negative: "[B]ecause the state of the law was not clearly established at the time the search in this case took place, the officers are entitled to the defense of qualified immunity." In what follows we excerpt the portion of the opinion dealing with the Fourth Amendment question.

CHIEF JUSTICE REHNQUIST delivered the opinion of the Court.

While executing an arrest warrant in a private home, police officers invited representatives of the media to accompany them. We hold that such a "media ride along" does violate the Fourth Amendment. . . .

In 1604, an English court made the now-famous observation that "the house of every one is to him as his castle and fortress, as well for his defense against injury and violence, as for his repose." In his *Commentaries on the Laws of England*, William Blackstone noted that

"the law of England has so particular and tender a regard to the immunity of a man's house, that it stiles it his castle, and will never suffer it to be violated with impunity: agreeing herein with the sentiments of antient Rome. . . . For this reason no doors can in general be broken open to execute any civil process; though, in criminal causes, the public safety supersedes the private."

The Fourth Amendment embodies this centuries-old principle of respect for the privacy of the home:

Our decisions have applied these basic principles of the Fourth Amendment to situations, like those in this case, in which police enter a home under the authority of an arrest warrant in order to take into custody the suspect named in the warrant. In *Payton v. New York* (1980), we noted that although clear in its protection of the home, the common-law tradition at the time of the drafting of the Fourth Amendment was ambivalent on the question of whether police could enter a home without a warrant. We were ultimately persuaded that the "overriding respect for the sanctity of the home that has been embedded in our traditions since the origins of the Republic" meant that absent a warrant or exigent circumstances, police could not enter a home to make an arrest. We decided that "an arrest warrant founded on probable cause implicitly carries with it the limited authority to enter a dwelling in which the suspect lives when there is reason to believe the suspect is within."

Here, of course, the officers had such a warrant, and they were undoubtedly entitled to enter the Wilson home in order to execute the arrest warrant for Dominic Wilson. But it does not necessarily follow that they were entitled to bring a newspaper reporter and a photographer with them. In *Horton v. California*, (1990), we held "[i]f the scope of the search exceeds that permitted by the terms of a validly issued warrant or the character of the relevant exception from the warrant requirement, the subsequent seizure is unconstitutional without more." While this does not mean that every police action while inside a home must be explicitly authorized by the text of the warrant, the Fourth Amendment does require that police actions in execution of a warrant be related to the objectives of the authorized intrusion, see *Arizona v. Hicks,* 480 U.S. 321, 325 (1987). Certainly the presence of reporters inside the home was not related to the objectives of the authorized intrusion. Respondents concede that the reporters did not engage in the execution of the warrant, and did not assist the police in their task. The reporters therefore were not present for any reason related to the justification for police entry into the home—the apprehension of Dominic Wilson.

This is not a case in which the presence of the third parties directly aided in the execution of the warrant. Where the police enter a home under the authority of a warrant to search for stolen property, the presence of third parties for the purpose of identifying the stolen property has long been approved by this Court and our common-law tradition. Respondents argue that the presence of the Washington Post reporters in the Wilsons' home nonetheless served a number of legitimate law enforcement purposes. They first assert that officers should be able to exercise reasonable discretion about when it would "further their law enforcement mission to permit members of the news media to accompany them in executing a warrant." But this claim ignores the importance of the right of residential privacy at the core of the Fourth Amendment. It may well be that media ride-alongs further the law enforcement objectives of the police in a general sense, but that is not the same as furthering the purposes of the search. Were such generalized "law enforcement objectives" themselves sufficient to trump the Fourth Amendment, the protections guaranteed by that Amendment's text would be significantly watered down.

Respondents next argue that the presence of third parties could serve the law enforcement purpose of publicizing the government's efforts to combat crime, and facilitate accurate reporting on law enforcement activities. There is certainly language in our opinions interpreting the First Amendment which points to the importance of "the press" in informing the general public about the administration of criminal justice. In *Cox Broadcasting Corp. v. Cohn*, 420 U.S. 469, 491–492 (1975), for example, we said "in a society in which each individual has but limited time and resources with which to observe at first hand the operations of his government, he relies necessarily upon the press to bring to him in convenient form the facts of those operations." No one could gainsay the truth of these observations, or the importance of the First Amendment in protecting press freedom from abridgment by the government. But the Fourth Amendment also protects a very important right, and in the present case it is in terms of that right that the media ride-alongs must be judged.

Surely the possibility of good public relations for the police is simply not enough, standing alone, to justify the ride-along intrusion into a private home. And even the need for accurate reporting on police issues in general bears no direct relation to the constitutional justification for the police intrusion into a home in order to execute a felony arrest warrant.

Finally, respondents argue that the presence of third parties could serve in some situations to minimize police abuses and protect suspects, and also to protect the safety of the officers. While it might be reasonable for police officers to themselves videotape home entries as part of a "quality control" effort to ensure that the rights of homeowners are being respected, or even to preserve evidence (noting the use of a "mounted video camera" to record the details of a routine traffic stop), such a situation is significantly different from the media presence in this case. The Washington Post reporters in the Wilsons' home were working on a story for their own purposes. They were not present for the purpose of protecting the officers, much less the Wilsons. A private photographer was acting for private purposes, as evidenced in part by the fact that the newspaper and not the police retained the photographs. Thus, although the presence of third parties during the execution of a warrant may in some circumstances be constitutionally permissible, the presence of *these* third parties was not.

The reasons advanced by respondents, taken in their entirety, fall short of justifying the presence of media inside a home. We hold that it is a violation of the Fourth Amendment for police to bring members of the media or other third parties into a home during the execution of a warrant when the presence of the third parties in the home was not in aid of the execution of the warrant. . . . For the foregoing reasons, the judgment of the Court of Appeals is affirmed.

It is so ordered.

CHAPTER 10

ATTORNEYS, TRIALS, AND PUNISHMENTS

GRAND JURY SELECTION

In *Powers v. Ohio* (1991) the Court ruled that criminal defendants can challenge the race-based exclusion of jurors through peremptory challenges whether or not the defendant and excluded jurors are the same race. *Campbell v. Ohio* raised a similar question: Do white defendants have standing to object to discrimination against blacks in the selection of grand jurors? Read this case in conjunction with the material on jury trials, pages 580–592.

Campbell v. Louisiana

_____ U.S. _____ (1998)

Vote: 7 (Breyer, Ginsburg, Kennedy, O'Connor, Rehnquist, Souter, Stevens)
    2 (Scalia, Thomas)
Opinion of the Court: Kennedy
Opinion Concurring in Part and Dissenting in Part: Thomas

In 1992 a grand jury in Evangeline Parish, Louisiana, indicted Terry Campbell on one count of murder. In response, Campbell, who is white, filed a motion to quash the indictment. He alleged that the grand jury was selected in a manner that violated several of his constitutional rights, including the Fourteenth Amendment's guarantee of equal protection. Specifically, Campbell argued that the selection of grand jury forepersons in Evangeline Parish was done in a racially biased manner. To support this argument, Campbell's attorney noted that, between January 1976 and August 1993, no black person served as a grand jury foreperson in the parish, despite the fact that 20 percent of the registered voters are black. The state did not refute this evidence.

The trial judge, however, refused to quash the indictment because "Campbell, being a white man accused of killing another white man," lacked standing to complain "where all of the forepersons were white." After Campbell was convicted and sentenced to life in prison without parole, he appealed to the Louisiana Court of Appeals. That court held in his favor, ruling that under the U.S. Supreme Court's decision in *Powers v. Ohio,* Campbell had standing to object to the alleged discrimination even though he is white. The Louisiana Supreme Court reversed and the case eventually worked its way to the U.S. Supreme Court.

JUSTICE KENNEDY delivered the opinion of the Court.

We must decide whether a white criminal defendant has standing to object to discrimination against black persons in the selection of grand jurors. Finding he has the requisite standing to raise equal protection and due process claims, we reverse and remand. . . .

As an initial matter, we note Campbell complains about more than discrimination in the selection of his grand jury foreperson; he alleges that discrimination shaped the composition of the grand jury itself. In the federal system and in most States which use grand juries, the foreperson is selected from the ranks of the already seated grand jurors. Under those systems, the title "foreperson" is bestowed on one of the existing grand jurors without any change in the grand jury's composition. In Louisiana, by contrast, the judge selects the foreperson from the grand jury venire before the remaining members of the grand jury have been chosen by lot. In addition to his other duties, the foreperson of the Louisiana grand jury has the same full voting powers as other grand jury members. As a result, when the Louisiana judge selected the foreperson, he also selected one member of the grand jury outside of the drawing system used to compose the balance of that body. These considerations require us to treat the case as one alleging discriminatory selection of grand jurors.

Standing to litigate often turns on imprecise distinctions and requires difficult line drawing. On occasion, however, we can ascertain standing with relative ease by applying rules established in prior cases. Campbell's equal protection claim is such an instance.

In *Powers v. Ohio* we found a white defendant had standing to challenge racial discrimination against black persons in the use of peremptory challenges. We determined the defendant himself could raise the equal protection rights of the excluded jurors. Recognizing our general reluctance to permit a litigant to assert the rights of a third party, we found three preconditions had been satisfied: (1) the defendant suffered an "injury in fact"; (2) he had a "close relationship" to the excluded jurors; and (3) there was some hindrance to the excluded jurors asserting their own rights. We concluded a white defendant suffers a serious injury in fact because discrimination at the voir dire stage " 'casts doubt on the integrity of the judicial process' . . . and places the fairness of a criminal proceeding in doubt." This cloud of doubt deprives the defendant of the certainty that a verdict in his case "is given in accordance with the law by persons who are fair." Second, the excluded juror and criminal defendant have a close relationship: They share a common interest in eliminating discrimination, and the criminal defendant has an incentive to serve as an effective advocate because a victory may result in over-turning his conviction. Third, given the economic burdens of litigation and the small financial reward available, "a juror dismissed because of race probably will leave the courtroom possessing little incentive to set in motion the arduous process needed to vindicate his own rights." Upon consideration of these factors, we concluded a white defendant had standing to bring an equal protection chal-lenge to racial discrimination against black persons in the petit jury selection process.

Although Campbell challenges discriminatory selection of grand jurors, rather than petit jurors, *Powers'* reasoning applies to this case on the question of stand-ing. Our prior cases have not decided whether a white defendant's own equal pro-tection rights are violated when the composition of his grand jury is tainted by dis-crimination against black persons. We do not need to address this issue because Campbell seeks to assert the well-established equal protection rights of black per-sons not to be excluded from grand jury service on the basis of their race. Campbell satisfies the three preconditions for third-party standing outlined in *Powers.*

Regardless of his or her skin color, the accused suffers a significant injury in fact when the composition of the grand jury is tainted by racial discrimination. "[D]iscrimination on the basis of race in the selection of members of a grand jury . . . strikes at the fundamental values of our judicial system" because the grand jury is a central component of the criminal justice process. The Fifth Amendment requires the Federal Government to use a grand jury to initiate a prosecution, and 22 States adopt a similar rule as a matter of state law. The grand jury, like the petit jury, "acts as a vital check against the wrongful exercise of power by the State and its prosecutors." It controls not only the initial decision to indict, but also signifi-cant decisions such as how many counts to charge and whether to charge a greater or lesser offense, including the important decision to charge a capital crime. The integrity of these decisions depends on the integrity of the process used to select the grand jurors. If that process is infected with racial discrimination, doubt is cast over the fairness of all subsequent decisions. *Powers* emphasized the harm inflict-ed when a prosecutor discriminates by striking racial minorities in open court and in front of the entire jury pool. The Court expressed concern that this tactic might encourage the jury to be lawless in its own actions. The State suggests this sort of harm is not inflicted when a single grand juror is selected based on racial preju-dice because the discrimination is invisible to the grand jurors on that panel; it only becomes apparent when a pattern emerges over the course of years. This argument, however, underestimates the seriousness of the allegations. In *Powers,* even if the prosecutor had been motivated by racial prejudice, those responsible for the defendant's fate, the judge and the jury, had shown no actual bias. If, by contrast, the allegations here are true, the impartiality and discretion of the judge himself would be called into question.

The remaining two preconditions to establish third party standing are satisfied with little trouble. We find no reason why a white defendant would be any less effective as an advocate for excluded grand jurors than for excluded petit jurors. The defendant and the excluded grand juror share a common interest in eradicating discrimination from the grand jury selection process, and the defendant has a vital interest in asserting the excluded juror's rights because his conviction may be overturned as a result. The State contends Campbell's connection to "the excluded class of . . . jurors . . . who were not called to serve . . . for the prior 16 1/2 years is tenuous, at best." This argument confuses Campbell's underlying claim with the evidence needed to prove it.

To assert the rights of those venirepersons who were excluded from serving on the grand jury in his case, Campbell must prove their exclusion was on account of intentional discrimination. He seeks to do so based on past treatment of similarly situated venirepersons in other cases, but this does not mean he seeks to assert those venirepersons' rights. As a final matter, excluded grand jurors have the same economic disincentives to assert their own rights as do excluded petit jurors. We find Campbell, like any other white defendant, has standing to raise an equal protection challenge to discrimination against black persons in the selection of his grand jury. . . .

The judgment of the Louisiana Supreme Court is reversed. The case is remanded for further proceedings not inconsistent with this opinion.

It is so ordered.

JUSTICE THOMAS, with whom JUSTICE SCALIA joins, concurring in part and dissenting in part.

I fail to understand how the rights of blacks excluded from jury service can be vindicated by letting a white murderer go free. Yet, in *Powers v. Ohio* (1991), the Court held that a white criminal defendant had standing to challenge his criminal conviction based upon alleged violations of the equal protection rights of black prospective jurors. Today's decision, rather than merely reaffirming *Powers'* misguided doctrine of third-party standing, applies that doctrine to a context in which even *Powers'* rationales are inapplicable. Because *Powers* is both incorrect as an initial matter and inapposite to the case at hand, I respectfully dissent from [part] of the Court's opinion.

Powers broke new ground by holding for the first time that a criminal defendant may raise an equal protection challenge to the use of peremptory strikes to exclude jurors of a different race. Recognizing that the defendant could not claim that his own equal protection rights had been denied, the Court held that the defendant had standing to assert the equal protection rights of veniremen excluded from the jury. The Court concluded that the defendant had such "third party standing" because three criteria had been met: he had suffered an "injury in fact"; he had a "close relation" to the excluded jurors; and there was "some hindrance" to the jurors' ability to protect their own interests.

Powers distorted standing principles and equal protection law, and should be overruled. As JUSTICE SCALIA explained at length in his dissent, the defendant in *Powers* could not satisfy even the first element of standing—injury in fact. The defendant, though certainly displeased with his conviction, failed to demonstrate that the alleged discriminatory use of peremptory challenges against veniremen of another race had any effect on the outcome of his trial. The Court instead found that the defendant had suffered a "cognizable" injury because racial discrimination in jury selection " 'casts doubt on the integrity of the judicial process' " and "invites cynicism respecting the jury's neutrality and its obligation to adhere to the law." But the severity of an alleged wrong and a perception of unfairness do not constitute injury in fact. Indeed, " '[i]njury in perception' would seem to be the very antithesis of 'injury in fact.' " (SCALIA, J., dissenting). Furthermore, there is no reason why a violation of a third party's right to serve on a jury should be grounds for reversal when other violations of third-party rights, such as obtaining evidence against the defendant in violation of another person's Fourth or Fifth Amendment rights, are not.

CHAPTER 11

DISCRIMINATION

EQUALITY IN WELFARE BENEFITS

In the 1969 case of *Shapiro v. Thompson,* the Court considered the question whether states could deny welfare assistance to residents who had lived in their jurisdictions for less than one year. The Court ruled that such laws violate the Fourteenth Amendment's Equal Protection Clause unless the state can show that they are necessary to promote a compelling governmental interest. In *Shapiro,* no such showing was made and the Court struck down the laws.

Saenz v. Roe seems to raise a similar question—but did the Court invoke the logic of *Shapiro* to answer it? To be sure, the majority cites *Shapiro.* Yet, one of the more interesting aspects of the case is the Court's use of the "previously dormant" Privileges or Immunities Clause of the Fourteenth Amendment. Does the majority make a compelling case for its reliance on this clause, or do you agree with the dissenters who argue that it may not have the meaning the Court ascribes to it?

Saenz v. Roe

_____ U.S. _____ (1999)
Vote: 7 (Breyer, Ginsburg, Kennedy, O'Connor, Scalia, Souter, Stevens)
2 (Rehnquist, Thomas)
Opinion of the Court: Stevens
Dissenting Opinions: Rehnquist, Thomas

In 1992 the California Legislature enacted §11450.03 of the state's Welfare and Institutions Code. That section— which sought to reduce the state's budget—limited new residents, for the first year they live in

California, to the welfare benefits they would have received in the state of their prior residence. In other words, the state established a two-tier welfare system: residents of a year or more would receive California's standard (and generous) benefits; newcomers (for the first year) would receive the benefits provided by the state from which they came.

The statute was challenged by several new California residents. Among them were Brenda Roe, who had moved with her husband to Long Beach, California, from Oklahoma, and Anna Doe, who had moved from Washington, D.C., when she was six months pregnant. Under the California statute the Roes would have received $307 per month rather than the $565 benefit given to in-state residents; for Doe, those figures were $330 and $454, respectively.

California did not dispute the contention that §11450.03 would create significant disparities between newcomers and welfare recipients who have resided in the state for more than one year. Rather, it relied on the undisputed fact that the statute would save some $10.9 million in annual welfare costs. It argued that this cost saving was an appropriate exercise of budgetary authority as long as the residency requirement did not penalize the right to travel.

A district court judge disagreed. Relying primarily on the Supreme Court's decision in *Shapiro v. Thompson* (1969), he concluded that the statute placed "a penalty on the decision of new residents to migrate to the State and be treated on an equal basis with existing residents."

JUSTICE STEVENS delivered the opinion of the Court.

The word "travel" is not found in the text of the Constitution. Yet the "constitutional right to travel from one State to another" is firmly embedded in our jurisprudence. Indeed, as Justice Stewart reminded us in *Shapiro v. Thompson,* 394 U.S. 618 (1969), the right is so important that it is "assertable against private interference as well as governmental action . . . a virtually unconditional personal right, guaranteed by the Constitution to us all." *Id.,* at 643 (concurring opinion).

In *Shapiro,* we reviewed the constitutionality of three statutory provisions that denied welfare assistance to residents of Connecticut, the District of Columbia, and Pennsylvania, who had resided within those respective jurisdictions less than one year immediately preceding their applications for assistance. Without pausing to identify the specific source of the right, we began by noting that the Court had long "recognized that the nature of our Federal Union and our constitutional concepts of personal liberty unite to require that all citizens be free to travel throughout the length and breadth of our land uninhibited by statutes, rules, or regulations which unreasonably burden or restrict this movement." We squarely held that it was "constitutionally impermissible" for a State to enact durational residency requirements for the purpose of inhibiting the migration by needy persons into the State. We further held that a classification that had the effect of imposing a penalty on the exercise of the right to travel violated the Equal Protection Clause "unless shown to be necessary to promote a *compelling* governmental interest," and that no such showing had been made.

In this case California argues that §11450.03 was not enacted for the impermissible purpose of inhibiting migration by needy persons and that, unlike the legislation reviewed in *Shapiro*, it does not penalize the right to travel because new arrivals are not ineligible for benefits during their first year of residence. California submits that, instead of being subjected to the strictest scrutiny, the statute should be upheld if it is supported by a rational basis and that the State's legitimate interest in saving over $10 million a year satisfies that test. . . . The debate about the appropriate standard of review, together with the potential relevance of the federal statute, persuades us that it will be useful to focus on the source of the constitutional right on which respondents rely.

The "right to travel" discussed in our cases embraces at least three different components. It protects the right of a citizen of one State to enter and to leave another State, the right to be treated as a welcome visitor rather than an unfriendly alien when temporarily present in the second State, and, for those travelers who elect to become permanent residents, the right to be treated like other citizens of that State.

It was the right to go from one place to another, including the right to cross state borders while en route, that was vindicated in *Edwards v. California,* (1941), which invalidated a state law that impeded the free interstate passage of the indigent. Given that §11450.03 imposed no obstacle to respondents' entry into California, we think the State is correct when it argues that the statute does not directly impair the exercise of the right to free interstate movement. For the purposes of this case, therefore, we need not identify the source of that particular right in the text of the Constitution. . . .

The second component of the right to travel is, however, expressly protected by the text of the Constitution. The first sentence of Article IV, §2, provides:

"The Citizens of each State shall be entitled to all Privileges and Immunities of Citizens in the several States."

Thus, by virtue of a person's state citizenship, a citizen of one State who travels in other States, intending to return home at the end of his journey, is entitled to enjoy the "Privileges and Immunities of Citizens in the several States" that he visits. This provision removes "from the citizens of each State the disabilities of alienage in the other States." It provides important protections for nonresidents who enter a State whether to obtain employment (1978), to procure medical services (1973), or even to engage in commercial shrimp fishing. Those protections are not "absolute," but the Clause "does bar discrimination against citizens of other States where there is no substantial reason for the discrimination beyond the mere fact that they are citizens of other States." There may be a substantial reason for requiring the nonresident to pay more than the resident for a hunting license or to enroll in the state university, see *Vlandis v. Kline*, 412 U.S. 441, 445 (1973), but our cases have not identified any acceptable reason for qualifying the protection afforded by the Clause for "the 'citizen of State A who ventures into State B' to settle there and establish a home." Permissible justifications for discrimination between residents and nonresidents are simply inapplicable to a nonresident's exercise of the right to move into another State and become a resident of that State.

What is at issue in this case, then, is this third aspect of the right to travel—the right of the newly arrived citizen to the same privileges and immunities enjoyed by other citizens of the same State. That right is protected not only by the new arrival's status as a state citizen, but also by her status as a citizen of the United States. That additional source of protection is plainly identified in the opening words of the Fourteenth Amendment:

"All persons born or naturalized in the United States, and subject to the jurisdiction thereof, are citizens of the United States and of the State wherein they reside. No State shall make or enforce any law which shall abridge the privileges or immunities of citizens of the United States; . . ." Despite fundamentally differing views concerning the coverage of the Privileges or Immunities Clause of the Fourteenth Amendment, most notably expressed in the majority and dissenting opinions in the *Slaughter-House Cases* (1873), it has always been common ground that this Clause protects the third component of the right to travel. Writing for the majority in the Slaughter-House Cases, Justice Miller explained that one of the privileges conferred by this Clause "is that a citizen of the United States can, of his own volition, become a citizen of any State of the Union by a *bona fide* residence therein, with the same rights as other citizens of that State." Justice Bradley, in dissent, used even stronger language to make the same point:

"The states have not now, if they ever had, any power to restrict their citizenship to any classes or persons. A citizen of the United States has a perfect constitutional right to go to and reside in any State he chooses, and to claim citizenship therein, and an equality of rights with every other citizen; and the whole power of the nation is pledged to sustain him in that right. He is not bound to cringe to any superior, or to pray for any act of grace, as a means of enjoying all the rights and privileges enjoyed by other citizens."

That newly arrived citizens "have two political capacities, one state and one federal," adds special force to their claim that they have the same rights as others who share their citizenship. Neither mere rationality nor some intermediate standard of review should be used to judge the constitutionality of a state rule that discriminates against some of its citizens because they have been domiciled in the State for less than a year. The appropriate standard may be more categorical than that articulated in *Shapiro*, but it is surely no less strict.

Because this case involves discrimination against citizens who have completed their interstate travel, the State's argument that its welfare scheme affects the right to travel only "incidentally" is beside the point. Were we concerned solely with actual deterrence to migration, we might be persuaded that a partial withholding of benefits constitutes a lesser incursion on the right to travel than an outright denial of all benefits. But since the right to travel embraces the citizen's right to be treated equally in her new State of residence, the discriminatory classification is itself a penalty. . . .

The classifications challenged in this case—and there are many—are defined entirely by (a) the period of residency in California and (b) the location of the prior residences of the disfavored class members. The favored class of beneficiaries includes all eligible California citizens who have resided there for at least one year, plus those new arrivals who last resided in another country or in a State that provides benefits at least as generous as California's. Thus, within the broad category of citizens who resided in California for less than a year, there are many who are treated like lifetime residents. And within the broad sub-category of new arrivals who are treated less favorably, there are many smaller classes whose benefit levels are determined by the law of the States from whence they came. To justify § 11450.03, California must therefore explain not only why it is sound fiscal policy to discriminate against those who have been citizens for less than a year, but also why it is permissible to apply such a variety of rules within that class.

These classifications may not be justified by a purpose to deter welfare applicants from migrating to California for three reasons. First, although it is reasonable to assume that some persons may be motivated to move for the purpose of obtaining higher benefits, the empirical evidence reviewed by the District Judge, which takes into account the high cost of living in California, indicates that the number of such persons is quite small—surely not large enough to justify a burden on those who had no such motive. Second, California has represented to the Court that the legislation was not enacted for any such reason. Third, even if it were, as we squarely held in *Shapiro v. Thompson* (1969), such a purpose would be unequivocally impermissible.

Disavowing any desire to fence out the indigent, California has instead advanced an entirely fiscal justification for its multitiered scheme. The enforcement of § 11450.03 will save the State approximately $10.9 million a year. The question is not whether such saving is a legitimate purpose but whether the State may accomplish that end by the discriminatory means it has chosen. An evenhanded, across-the-board reduction of about 72 cents per month for every beneficiary would produce the same result. But our negative answer to the question does not rest on the weakness of the State's purported fiscal justification. It rests on the fact that the Citizenship Clause of the Fourteenth Amendment expressly equates citizenship with residence: "That Clause does not provide for, and does not allow for, degrees of citizenship based on length of residence." It is equally clear that the Clause does not tolerate a hierarchy of 45 subclasses of similarly situated citizens based on the location of their prior residence. Thus § 11450.03 is doubly vulnerable: Neither the duration of respondents' California residence, nor the identity of their prior States of residence, has any relevance to their need for benefits. Nor do those factors bear any relationship to the State's interest in making an equitable allocation of the funds to be distributed among its needy citizens. As in *Shapiro*, we reject any contributory rationale for the denial of benefits to new residents:

"But we need not rest on the particular facts of these cases. Appellants' reasoning would logically permit the State to bar new residents from schools, parks, and libraries or deprive them of police and fire protection. Indeed it would permit the State to apportion all benefits and services according to the past tax contributions of its citizens." In short, the State's legitimate interest in saving money provides no justification for its decision to discriminate among equally eligible citizens. . . .

Citizens of the United States, whether rich or poor, have the right to choose to be citizens "of the State wherein they reside." The States, however, do not have any right to select their citizens. The Fourteenth Amendment, like the Constitution itself, was, as Justice Cardozo put it, "framed upon the theory that the peoples of the several states must sink or swim together, and that in the long run prosperity and salvation are in union and not division." The judgment of the Court of Appeals is affirmed.

It is so ordered.

CHIEF JUSTICE REHNQUIST, with whom JUSTICE THOMAS joins, dissenting.

The Court today breathes new life into the previously dormant Privileges or Immunities Clause of the Fourteenth Amendment—a Clause relied upon by this Court in only one other decision, *Colgate v. Harvey* (1935), overruled five years later by *Madden v. Kentucky* (1940). It uses this Clause to strike down what I believe is a reasonable measure falling under the head of a "good-faith residency requirement." Because I do not think any provision of the Constitution—and surely not a provision relied upon for only the second time since its enactment 130 years ago—requires this result, I dissent.

JUSTICE THOMAS, with whom the Chief Justice joins, dissenting.

I join The Chief Justice's dissent. I write separately to address the majority's conclusion that California has violated "the right of the newly arrived citizen to the same privileges and immunities enjoyed by other citizens of the same State." *Ante*, at 12. In my view, the majority attributes a meaning to the Privileges or Immunities Clause that likely was unintended when the Fourteenth Amendment was enacted and ratified. . . .

As The Chief Justice points out, it comes as quite a surprise that the majority relies on the Privileges or Immunities Clause at all in this case. That is because the *Slaughter-House* Cases sapped the Clause of any meaning. Although the majority appears to breathe new life into the Clause today, it fails to address its historical underpinnings or its place in our constitutional jurisprudence. Because I believe that the demise of the Privileges or Immunities Clause has contributed in no small part to the current disarray of our Fourteenth Amendment jurisprudence, I would be open to reevaluating its meaning in an appropriate case. Before invoking the Clause, however, we should endeavor to understand what the framers of the Fourteenth Amendment thought that it meant. We should also consider whether the Clause should displace, rather than augment, portions of our equal protection and substantive due process jurisprudence. The majority's failure to consider these important questions raises the specter that the Privileges or Immunities Clause will become yet another convenient tool for inventing new rights, limited solely by the "predilections of those who happen at the time to be Members of this Court." I respectfully dissent.